MODELLING
HEAVY INDUSTRY
A Guide for Railway Modellers

MODELLING HEAVY INDUSTRY

A Guide for Railway Modellers

ARTHUR ORMROD

THE CROWOOD PRESS

First published in 2017 by
The Crowood Press Ltd
Ramsbury, Marlborough
Wiltshire SN8 2HR

www.crowood.com

British Library Cataloguing-in-Publication Data
A catalogue record for this book is available from the British Library.

ISBN 978 1 78500 337 0

Disclaimer
The author and the publisher do not accept any responsibility in
any manner whatsoever for any error or omission, or any loss,
damage, injury, adverse outcome, or liability of any kind incurred
as a result of the use of any of the information contained in this
book, or reliance upon it. If in doubt about any aspect of railway
modelling skills and techniques, readers are advised to seek
professional advice.

Designed and typeset by Guy Croton
Publishing Services, Maidstone, Kent

Printed and bound in India by Parkson's Graphics

CONTENTS

PREFACE

My involvement with railways and railway modelling follows a pattern similar to many. One of the Baby Boomer generation, I was brought up with the steam railway as an everyday experience. Living in the Manchester area, my friends and I were exposed to a busy and vibrant railway environment. If I say that Patricroft station and locomotive depot were just a mile away, that will give many an idea of the nature of the local railway with which I was familiar. Spare time was spent kicking a football, playing cricket with wickets drawn on a wall, building carts and dens, and observing the local railway scene. Not surprisingly, for some of us, that exposure turned into a lifelong fascination with railways and their operations. Soon, railway-themed presents at Christmas and birthdays translated into a train set, Hornby Dublo 3 rail, which initiated a parallel interest in model railways. That interest waxed and waned over the years, yet was always there, in the background, emerging more strongly than ever in later years.

Much of this railway interest was against a backdrop of industry, and industry was, as with the railways, everywhere. A hundred yards from my front door stood the factory of Gardner's diesel engines; a mile to the south was the sprawling and bustling Trafford Park industrial estate complete with its own railway system; a couple of miles to the north lay the former Manchester Collieries' network of railways and pits, then part of the NCB; to the west were the chimneys and furnaces of the Lancashire Steel Corporation. These complex and sprawling plants and operations always fascinated me, and working briefly at Lancashire Steel at Irlam near Manchester, and then at Shotton Steelwoks on Deeside, both by then part of the British Steel Corporation, sparked a particular interest in the iron and steel industry.

It was perhaps fate, then, that my modelling interests should have always included plans to incorporate some elements of these industries in my own layouts. Though my own plans are directed largely, though certainly not exclusively, towards the iron and steel industry, and are ambitious in size, the contents of this book are very much aimed at any modeller who might wish to incorporate representations of any industry into their layout, even in the smallest of spaces.

CHAPTER ONE

INTRODUCTION

WHAT IS HEAVY INDUSTRY?

Heavy industry and the railways are closely connected and usually adjacent, yet the great majority of the scenery included in railway models is non-industrial in nature beyond the actual railway infrastructure: houses, towns, villages and the rural landscape. This book seeks to redress the balance by showing how to build realistic models of the kind of heavy industry that appeared so often, and still does, alongside the railway network.

A dictionary or online resource will define heavy industry in economic terms as an industry with a high capital investment, one with a high cost of entry. Your local bank manager is not going to lend you enough money to build a steelworks, a large engineering enterprise or an oil refinery, as you would need to raise several millions to build something that would justify the description of 'heavy industry'. On the ground, and for the modeller, that translates to extensive plant, large buildings and structures, and at least a rail link if not an internal railway system.

I suspect, though, that when most people read the phrase 'heavy industry', it is not the economic definition that springs to mind but a vision of cavernous black sheds, tall chimneys and large structures silhouetted against the skyline.

There are still examples of heavy industry scattered about the UK: engineering, vehicle manufacturers, oil and petrochemical plants and steelworks. They are, however, becoming increasingly difficult to find. In October 2015, over a hundred years of iron and steelmaking came to an end on Teesside with the closure of the Redcar works. During the period in which this book was being written, the fate of the steelworks at Port

Archetypal heavy industry: a panoramic view across part of Port Talbot Steelworks sometime around 1960. Cavernous buildings, tall chimneys, towering structures, conveyor belts and internal railways all feature in this image. TATA STEEL EUROPE

An official photograph showing bogie ore hoppers being loaded at Port Talbot. Once loaded they would have been hauled 50 miles (80km) to Llanwern Steelworks, a service that at one time saw triple heading by three class 37s. Block movements of materials like ore and coal have been a staple of railway operations since their inception. TATA STEEL EUROPE

Talbot hung in the balance. As I was drawing the manuscript to a conclusion, news broke that indicated that, pending some negotiations over pension arrangements, the works might be saved, at least for a further five years, whilst receiving several billions in investment. It was a stark reminder of what we have and how quickly things can be lost.

HEAVY INDUSTRY AND THE RAILWAYS

For the railway modeller, heavy industry has a lot to offer: as a dramatic backdrop to mainline operations, to provide a reason for goods' traffic and as a railway scene in its own right. Built in low relief along the rear of the baseboard, as some later examples will show, large industrial structures can not only provide an imposing backdrop to model railway operations,

but also obviate the need to provide a painted, two-dimensional backscene. This is something some modeller's struggle with. It is very easy to fill a corner with interesting buildings and to help lose that jarring right-angled joint.

Real railways don't run aimlessly to and fro, nor round and round. Their function is to provide a transport service. Over the years, heavy industry has been an essential customer providing very large volumes and endless flows of incoming raw materials and outgoing finished goods. Some industries have demanded specialist vehicles, many available as ready-to-run models or as kits, and the provision of an appropriate industry will justify their operation. Block trains, in particular, do not originate in rural goods' yards nor run to single-siding factories; they run between large industrial facilities, moving materials in vast quantities.

THE SCOPE OF THIS BOOK

The aim of this book is to be a 'How to' guide for modelling heavy industry and it is very much 'how I *actually* did it' rather than 'this is how you *might* do it'. The buildings and structures have actually been built and the chapters recount the steps in construction and how any problems encountered were overcome. One chapter looks at tools, including some not found in the average toolkit, and at the basic materials and adhesives that have been used. A further chapter considers the prototype using a selection of photographs with extended descriptions.

The bulk of the book consists of chapters recounting the building of particular structures or plant. Though many of these projects will reflect my own interest in the iron and steel industry, they will cover building types and techniques that will enable any modeller to assemble many types of large industrial buildings and plant. One chapter looks at those features that have a general application and that might be repeated on buildings of various types, e.g. chimneys and pipework. The models were built for my own purposes and are intended as components for a model of a large, integrated steelworks that will be housed in a purpose-built outbuilding. My chosen scale is 4mm/ft, so all of the builds are to that scale. Owing to the sheer size of some of the prototypes, few of the projects are built to true scale and they incorporate elements of selective compression. The 4mm modeller is blessed with the largest range of commercial support for kits, buildings and parts, and I have made full use of them and also of the equally large range available to the H0 modeller.

The modeller in N or 2mm scale will find a good number of these parts available too, particularly from the Continental and US-based suppliers. At the time of writing, the US company Walthers seems to have much more of its Cornerstone range of industrial structures available in N than in H0.

Having said that, the bulk of the modelling in this book is concerned with the use of basic raw materials, and where kits or commercially available parts have been used, it was largely to speed up the process. I wouldn't consider, for example, making up an open stairway when there are perfectly good components available from Plastruct. Still, there is nothing that could not have been made from scratch in foamboard, styrene or brass, had a commercial part not been available. When you are undertaking a very large project, any time-saving steps are always worth considering.

RESEARCHING THE PROTOTYPE

It is possible to visit a well-stocked railway bookshop and buy a volume on the most obscure branchline, the most insignificant goods' wagon or the most arcane detail of uniform buttons. Even with these riches of published resources, modeller's still often struggle to find the complete information needed to accurately complete their project. Despite the availability of seemingly all and any information on railway history, both the letter pages of the magazines and internet forums fizz with arguments over many aspects of detail.

Enter the world of modelling heavy industry and the riches available to the railway modeller evaporate almost completely. Whereas there are five or so model railway magazines, half-a-dozen prototype railway magazines, several special interest magazines and a seemingly endless supply of new railway-themed books, there is virtually no hobby interest in heavy industry to justify the publication of a single related book or magazine. *Archive Magazine* is perhaps the closest, covering a range of subjects and very often including articles on heavy industry.

Technical books are available, sometimes at great cost, but they rarely contain the type of information and photographs of use to the modeller. Much less so these days, books were once published aimed at the general public, at young boys in particular, along the lines of *The Wonder of Steel* or *Where Does Our Coal Come From?* Between the 1930s and 1960s there seemed to be a much greater level of interest amongst the general public about the industry and processes they saw around them. Some companies have published promotional material, often well illustrated, displaying their plant and processes to the general public. Trade magazines feature illustrated articles on new plant and their advertising pages often have good photographs of machinery and equipment. Used book shops, Abebooks and eBay are good sources to find such materials though it involves much searching in the dark, just to see what there is.

Most large industrial concerns employed either a works' photographer or contracted one in, to record aspects of their operations and of new developments and investments. These professionally produced images are crystal clear, and illustrate the buildings, plant and equipment. If you can find them, they are an invaluable source of information. Sadly, it is likely that thousands upon thousands of such images have been lost over the years as companies have merged or ceased trading. Some have found their way into online archives. The Canmore Collection contains a huge amount of historic information and photographs, covering industry and other subjects in Scotland (canmore.org.uk). Another is the British Steel Collection containing photographs of steel manufacturing in the north-east (www.britishsteelcollection.org.uk). Over the years I have amassed a good collection of such images, largely related to the iron and steel industry, and some feature in this volume.

I will mention the German photographers and academics, Bernd and Hiller Becher, who for several years travelled across Europe and the United States photographing large industrial structures. Many of their images, again monochrome, have been published in large-format hardback books, generally with one image per page. Captions are minimal, just location, country and year, and versions in English, German and French have appeared. Many focus on one topic and examples include 'Blast Furnaces', 'Cooling Towers', 'Gas Tanks (Holders)' and 'Water Towers'. The images are of the highest quality, very clear and they focus entirely on a single industrial plant. Sounds almost too good to be true you may say – well, yes. They are considered as 'art' books and are priced as such. When out of print, certain volumes have sold for several hundreds of pounds.

However, occasionally bargains do turn up and they are well worth having a look at.

Internet searches can reveal other online resources, archives and special-interest pages, and searching for images, in particular, can unearth some useful information.

SPACE, HEIGHT AND PROPORTION

A common perception is that to convincingly model heavy industry, the modeller needs lots of space and, should ambitions stretch to it, a barn could be filled, yet still not be sufficient to model one of the larger industrial sites in full. In fact, a 4mm model of Llanwern Steelworks as originally built, roughly 2 x ½ mile would measure 40 x 10m. When officially opened in 1962, Llanwern covered a very large area and being a relatively modern development it was established on a greenfield site incorporating plenty of space for further growth. Fortunately, for the modeller at least, many of our industrial enterprises had much older origins and were established on relatively small sites. By the 1960s and 1970s these sites had become cramped and new buildings and developments had been squeezed in, cheek by jowl – a feature that is a blessing to the space-starved modeller.

However much space is available, most railway modeller's live and work with the concept of selective compression, taking the essence of the real railway scene and squeezing it into the space available. As mentioned, the steelworks' projects covered in this book are part of a plan to model the key elements of an integrated steelworks and an L-shaped area of approximately 18 x 5ft (5.5 x 1.5m) with a 5 x 3ft (1.5 x 1m) arm has been allocated – a large enough area by most modellers' standards but still one requiring a high degree of selective compression. Within that scheme, several of the individual elements would themselves provide a standalone industry and would fit into considerably smaller areas. Some examples of model industry taking up no more than an inch or so along the rear of the layout will be considered, as will others that would neatly fit into a corner.

A cramped industrial site with railway lines showing just how tight curves used in industry can be. TATA STEEL EUROPE

ABSOLUTE SCALE

The modeller committed to absolute scale modelling, taking prototype measurements and reducing them down to their chosen scale, will not need to angst over selective compression. The dimensions to work to are given; prototypes too large to scale down to the available space cannot be considered. To the absolute scale modeller the discussion in the next section is possibly irrelevant, though the curious question of scale height should at least be considered.

However, for those modellers prepared to make some sacrifice in true scale, there are decisions to be made about how best to balance the compression required.

SPACE

The first question for the modeller is 'how much space do I have and how much am I prepared to devote to industrial modelling?'. Only the individual can answer this question and once answered, a footprint for each structure can be determined.

A corner of my Staplegrove module showing a railway line squeezed between buildings.

Even a 250ft (76m) chimney just does not look right on a small diorama.

Generally speaking, to capture the essence of heavy industry, one large building might look better than two smaller ones in the same space. Consideration should also be given to the possibility of modelling only selected parts of buildings by merging them into the backscene. If an internal railway system is to be incorporated, this will place some demands for a minimal space and limitations on the positioning of buildings, though the prototype has been kind to us. Sharp curves, tight clearances and buildings cut back to give way to railway traffic abound. Indeed, incorporating sharper curvatures on your industrial lines help distinguish them from the main lines.

HEIGHT

Height, particularly of very tall structures, presents a curious dilemma and a number of other writers have commented on this peculiarity. If a strictly scale model of an actual building or a tree is being modelled, then the height will be dictated. However, tall objects built to scale often just do not look right and can look too tall, too dominant.

We see tall features, trees and buildings, from the ground and, looking up at them, they seem to diminish as they soar away from us. Their great height compared to the smaller buildings, vehicles and rolling stock around is somehow lost. It is quite difficult at ground-level to fully appreciate the height of such structures. Conversely, on a model we either look down on tall structures or view them side on. Their tops are closer than the railway and rolling stock beneath them, as they loom up into view. We are viewing the scene in an unusual manner and their height is somehow accentuated, whilst the rolling stock below is diminished.

The other consideration is the relationship of scale height to ground space. A measurement that would be considered as tall is nothing as a measurement along the ground. The blast furnace at Redcar, 100m tall, towers over surrounding structures. Standing at its base, the observer would soon get a stiff neck staring up at it. Yet 100m is nothing as a measurement on the ground.

The viewer sees tall structures in contrast to the enormity of the landscape. Now in the limited areas that modeller's have available, scale-height structures often look well out of proportion. As long ago as 1859, an industrial chimney in Glasgow reached 138.4m (454ft) in height and today a height of 150m (492ft) is far from unusual and there are many very much taller. That chimney at Port Dundas, Glasgow, would be 908mm tall in 2mm scale and 1,816mm in 4mm scale. Try placing a suitable length of tubing vertically on a layout. It will look enormous, dwarfing to a most unrealistic degree everything else on the layout. You will probably be surprised at just how far it soars up above from the baseboard.

Of course, there are very many smaller chimneys but those serving the types of industry we are considering tend to be at least 50m or 160ft, and usually more, in height.

PROPORTION

Bringing these two dimensions together, area and height, leads on to the question of proportion and here there is no definitive answer. It has to look right. Waterless gas-holders, covered in Chapter 6, are always taller than they are wide. That is a characteristic feature of them and a model not sharing that relative proportion will be unconvincing. Measurements taken from several photographs of the prototype suggested that, typically, their width is about 60 per cent of their height. A model, irrespective of its general size, should adhere to this proportion. By taking the ground space available for the model, and using it with this 60 per cent figure, an appropriate height for a model can be determined. Or, if the model is planned to be a certain height, then the 60 per cent figure can determine its width. Drawing up a small table will give a range of options and making some simple mock-ups will help give a good sense of how well it all works.

My own project will incorporate several prototypically tall structures, chimneys, a gas-holder, a cooling tower, blast furnaces, along with some large buildings. I wanted to get the relative heights right, so I drew up a table with the heights of some typical prototype structures and from that worked out a range of heights for the corresponding models. I decided that the two coke-oven chimneys would be the tallest structures. Prototypes were typically in the order of 76m high, which in 4mm would scale out to around 1,000mm tall. I considered that this would look too tall and so decided on a height of 750mm. With that set as the tallest structure, I could then determine the heights of other structures.

These principles will be seen in practice with the model projects covering the cooling tower and gas-holder, in particular.

THE PROJECT MODELS

Finally, the planned model railway, which will incorporate the steelworks, will be housed in a dedicated building. As that building will not be erected until 2017, the models are currently being built on small, individual baseboards. Most of these boards are 10mm foamboard constructions and the intention is to fit these into the main boards as layout construction develops. Being foamboard they can easily be trimmed if required.

As a consequence, the models, as photographed, sit in isolation and are not yet integrated into a whole. One or two of the larger projects, the open-hearth melting shop, for example, sit on more substantial mini-baseboards with plywood framing. These will form part of a jigsaw of boards that will interlock and rest on a sub-baseboard. There is a plan for the overall steelworks' layout but the individual boards and tracks upon them have been built with the likelihood that some tweaking will be necessary and that some changes may be made as things develop.

CHAPTER TWO

THE PROTOTYPE

INTRODUCTION

We'll look at a number of photographs of structures and scenes typically associated with heavy industry in this chapter. They range in date from the 1950s to the present day, with a balance towards the earlier years. That is partly because my collection naturally reflects my own interest in the era and partly because we have lost so much of the infrastructure that finding modern photographs is not so easy. A good example of the difficulty in obtaining photographs is the gas-holder. Not that long ago, even small towns had one or two, and finding an example to photograph was not at all difficult. Trying to find one today is not so simple. To obtain a photograph of a traditional, framed gas-holder to illustrate the relevant chapter in this book, involved a detour off the M6 to Aston in Birmingham; even then only the frame survives. The actual gas-holding tank has long since been removed. An attempt to find the remains of a frameless gas-holder in Nottingham proved fruitless as there was only waste ground where it had stood until relatively recently.

Another difficulty with obtaining prototype photographs is that the sites of heavy industry are generally securely fenced off. The observer of the scene can, at best, only obtain photographs 'over the fence' or from a distance. It wasn't until I went around trying to photograph some contemporary industrial sites that I also realized just how much vegetation and foliage has been allowed to grow along the perimeters of many sites. Either by neglect, or more likely by a desire to develop some screening, trees and shrubs have been allowed to proliferate and can make photography difficult. Trying to obtain a photograph of bullet gas-holders proved very difficult. A site just off the M32 in Bristol proved impossible to get close enough to even to see them, let alone obtain a photograph. I recalled a set from many years ago at Partington, west of Manchester, and Google Earth showed them still there, at least when that image had been taken. They were there when I subsequently visited but I could only obtain an image over the fence and with other objects in the foreground.

Official sources, where they are available, provide the best photographs of the buildings and plant within the works' boundaries. Even industries that allow escorted visits for the public often have bans on photography, which may be enforced to varying degrees. The one heavy industry that is the exception in this respect is the railway network. Provided as a service to the public, and winding its way across our towns and countryside, we have an unparalleled access to much of it to observe and photograph. This ready access helps account for the very large number of photographs, magazines and books that are devoted to our railway history.

I have been collecting official photographs of the steel industry for some while and several of them feature in this volume to illustrate the prototype. Many of them are black and white, which reflects the use of this medium by the official and professional photographers of the day. What they lack in colour, they more than make up for in clarity.

PHOTOGRAPHS IN DETAIL

Good photographs of industrial sites can provide a wealth of detail, information and inspiration. I've selected fifteen photographs that span the years and that were taken at a number of sites. The sites featured all demonstrate that defining feature of heavy industry: large, complex and costly infrastructure. Let's have a look at them and see what they reveal to the modeller.

Margam Exchange sidings. Railways and heavy industry have long had a close relationship. TATA STEEL EUROPE

Steelworks – Panorama 1. There are several structures here that help to identify this as an iron and steelworks. TATA STEEL EUROPE

MARGAM EXCHANGE SIDINGS

If ever proof were needed of the close inter-dependency between the railways and heavy industry, then the photograph of the exchange sidings at Port Talbot Steelworks is it. The photograph features siding after siding with a capacity of several hundred wagons and, just visible to the right, a works' locomotive propelling a train. The railways provided the essential large-scale transport required and heavy industry, in turn, provided much of the traffic. With the serried ranks of mineral wagons, this particular photograph also illustrates the importance of the coal industry: more traffic for the railways and essential fuel for industry. To the left midground stand some tall wagon tipplers and across the back are chimneys, blast furnaces and, in the centre, a large, waterless gas-holder. This is still a very large industrial operation today, though its coal is now imported and delivered by sea.

STEELWORKS – PANORAMA 1

The next photograph is a panoramic view dated 1958 of the Lancashire Steel Corporation's Irlam works, situated on the north bank of the Manchester Ship Canal, between Manchester and Warrington. In common with much of the UK's steel industry, the works underwent much modernization and rebuilding in the post-war years. The first point to note is the neatly trimmed lawns and well-maintained kerbs and roadways in the foreground. Where space was available, many companies tried to provide a bit of greenery. At Irlam the scene in the photograph greeted visitors to the works, the main gate and offices being just behind the photographer. It was not all universally grim; though it should be said that the further a visitor delved into the works, the grimmer it got.

The two buildings at the left foreground were the newly built staff canteen and, behind it, the garage.

Sweeping left to right across the background is a concrete cooling tower in front of which stand three benzole scrubbers, then two waterless gas-holders: the near one, of 1 million cubic feet capacity, holding blast furnace gas and, behind it, one of 3 million cubic feet capacity, holding coke oven gas. Barely visible, at their feet, is the brick-built works' laboratory and above it, in the background murk, is the outline of the No. 1 blast furnace. Three others hide behind the gas-holders. The first of a number of tall, steel chimneys stands a little to the right. Panning further across are the dark outlines of the power-house and No. 1 steel melting shop, partly obscured behind a water tank supported on a tall, structural steel frame. The brick building in the midground is the works' canteen and to the right are the big black sheds of the rod and bar mill. Above the mill, two more steel chimneys reach skyward serving the No. 2 steel melting shop.

A railway line curves in from the right and disappears into the heart of the works. A number of figures can be seen going about their business and there are one or two small buildings visible: a shed and two corrugated metal sheds to the right. Bits of equipment, such as a wheelbarrow, some cable drums and a number of signposts, lie about the scene. Wires stretch between posts and buildings, and pipework on gantries passes across the view.

This extended description is to give an idea of the very wide variety of buildings and structures that can be present at a single site. These are steelworks' buildings but many might be suitable for other industries that the modeller may wish to replicate. Some of them are very large and complex, whilst others are as small and simple as a wooden shed. The projects in this book will cover a number of them.

STEELWORKS – PANORAMA 2

Next there is another general view of the Irlam works shown from the opposite direction to the view in the previous photograph. Railway lines run unfenced across the site with pipework on tall towers striding across the view. The works' offices are just visible in the middle background; to the right, a 12t covered railway van is present, while to the left stands a Bedford S Series tipper lorry. The Bedford S type, sometimes known as the 'Big Bedford', was a very common sight on British roads at the time.

Steelworks – Panorama 2. Conversely, though this is the same site, nothing here identifies the nature of the works. TATA STEEL EUROPE

GREENGATE & IRWELL 1

As a contrast, the next two photographs illustrate the 1950-built factory of Greengate & Irwell, which stood in Salford, not that far from the old Manchester Exchange Station, and which was visible to passengers on trains entering or leaving from the west. It is a medium-sized industrial plant, though elsewhere there were some very large buildings constructed in this manner, and it demonstrates a once common form of industrial building structure. The building has a structural skeleton of reinforced concrete beams, with the open faces filled in with plain and functional brickwork and metal-framed windows. Concrete lintels span the windows and there is a parapet around the flat roof.

GREENGATE & IRWELL 2

The functional exterior is enlivened with doorways, ladders, fire escapes and bits of industrial plant sitting on the roof. This type of build is referred to as 'brick curtain-wall construction'; the brickwork forming a curtain between the concrete, or alternatively steel, structural members. A building of this type is available in the Walthers Cornerstone range, the Geo. Roberts Printing Company building, available in H0 and N. Though not covered in this volume, this type of building could readily be constructed using some of the techniques outlined.

INDUSTRIAL OFFICES

The curvaceous works' office block illustrated next was that of Mitchell & Shackleton's on Green Lane, Patricroft, Manchester, so attractive a prototype that I know of at least two models already inspired by it and one day I'll add a third of my own. Mitchell & Shackleton's made medium-sized crankshafts for use in marine and stationary diesel engines. Heavy industry is not all gloomy industrial sheds; it incorporates a whole host of building types and functions. A building

RIGHT: *Industrial Offices. Mitchell & Shackleton's offices were a stylish example of industrial architecture proving that it's not all grim functionality.*

Greengate & Irwell 1. An example of curtain-wall construction.

Greengate & Irwell 2. Concrete windowsills and lintels, along with steel window frames (as featured on this building), are very common features on industrial buildings built in the middle years of the twentieth century.

Big black sheds. Large, anonymous sheds are a signal feature of heavy industry, housing all sorts of activities.

housing the offices and administration functions is near universal at any site of heavy industry. As with this example, they could be stylish examples of contemporary architecture.

BIG BLACK SHEDS

From the same position as the photograph above but panning to the left is one of those large, industrial sheds, perhaps the signal feature of heavy industry. This is a large, anonymous building, which could house any manner of industrial activity; here it was a machine shop. The works had closed by the time these photographs were taken, hence the boarded-up security lodge to the left and the rampant weed growth. Features of interest, along with the lodge, are the clerestory vent on the roof and various smaller structures, downpipes and some rusty steelwork alongside the large building.

My grandfather worked here as a centre lathe turner when I was a boy. On more than one occasion I was taken into the works by my grandmother, into the machine shop where he worked, to take in something he had forgotten. That would never be allowed today.

Interesting but unknown. This building, which once stood in Stoke-on-Trent, is not large but is full of interesting details and features.

INTERESTING BUT UNKNOWN

I have absolutely no idea what the purpose of the building in the next photograph was, nor who owned it. I photographed it around 1990 in Stoke-on-Trent just because it was such an interesting structure. Is it some form of power house and what is the purpose of that extended asbestos clad roof and overhang? I suspect that I will never know, but one day I will construct a model of it and it will be given some suitable role.

AERIAL PHOTOGRAPHS

Returning next to the steel industry, we have an aerial photograph of the steelworks at Margam. Following a huge expansion project in the years following World War II, the works became better known as Port Talbot. This photograph shows the new blast furnace plant, which had been built in the 1940s and 1950s on the site of the original 1918 Margam furnaces. From front to rear there is the wharf, the ore stocking grounds spanned by a large ore bridge crane and the three blast furnaces. Behind them stands the open-hearth melting shop with its row of chimneys and, at the rear, the coke ovens. To the right foreground are buildings associated with ore processing and behind them the power house with its stubby chimneys.

Recently the 'Britain from Above' project has made available online an enormous number of aerial photographs of the UK taken over many years. They form a marvellous resource for anyone researching our industrial and railway past. Enter 'Britain from Above' into an internet search engine and an enormous archive of marvellous images becomes available.

CLUTTER AND DETAIL

The photograph of the Margam coke-ovens shows the reinforced-concrete construction of the service bunkers. In a later chapter the construction of a coal-blending plant is covered. On the prototype, that plant would send its coal on a conveyor belt up to the top of such service bunkers. This photograph includes some details of the pipework, gantries and conveyors that clutter many industrial sites. It has been included to illustrate just how much work can be involved in modelling heavy industry, especially with the smaller details that tie everything together.

LARGE INDUSTRIAL PLANT

We move on to a 1955 photograph showing the then newly erected No. I blast furnace at Lancashire Steel's Irlam works. The furnace has been blown in

Aerial photographs. Thousands of aerial images are now available online; they are an invaluable resource and usually show the layout of the internal railway system. TATA STEEL EUROPE

Clutter and detail. Modelling heavy industry can be demanding in both time and materials, there is a lot of it. TATA STEEL EUROPE

Large industrial plant. This blast furnace again gives an idea of the amount of detail that is often found in heavy industry. TATA STEEL EUROPE

and is working, although some cladding has still to be added to the structural framework of the cast house. One of the work's locomotive fleet, a Yorkshire Engine Company DE2 0-4-0DE, stands in the cast house coupled, via a spacer wagon, to a slag ladle and into which slag is being run. The site here was fairly cramped, with newer and generally larger plant being shoehorned into the site of older plant. The other challenge faced by management and workers was to keep production running whilst removing and replacing the equipment.

AN INDUSTRIAL BACK ROAD

The dirt and grime associated with much heavy industry is evidenced in the next photograph taken in the vicinity of the Irlam coke-ovens, which stand behind the right shoulder of the photographer. The concrete buildings to the left are associated with the coal-handling facilities and the building straight ahead, with its conveyors, is part of the ore-handling plant. This photograph is included to give the feel of one of the backwaters of a large industrial site. It includes a rail line or siding with some mineral wagons

An industrial back road. Just an obscure corner of a large works with steel mineral wagons providing the railway interest.
TATA STEEL EUROPE

patiently waiting who knows what. This photograph illustrates an interesting feature of some older and well-established industrial plants, the steel industry in particular. Many of these sites were established before the huge expansion in road transport from the 1950s onwards. They were built to be almost totally reliant on rail transport for both external and internal transport needs. Internal roadways were, if present at all, often rudimentary as there was very little traffic to use them. By the 1950s and 1960s, this was rapidly changing and many works struggled to find the space to squeeze in new roads as the need for them arose. Lancashire Steel was no different and in the middle of this photograph a muddy, puddle-strewn roadway winds between buildings and railway tracks. Elsewhere the company was building proper concrete roads with kerbs and drainage, and in its turn, this road too was upgraded.

AN INDUSTRIAL PANORAMA

This photograph, full of industrial interest and detail, shows the former Richard, Thomas & Baldwin's iron foundry at Landore, Llanelli. This well-established operation re-melted pig iron and produced iron castings, many for use within the steel industry itself. For Richard Thomas and Baldwins (RTB), and later for the British Steel Corporation (BSC), it

cast, amongst other things, ingot moulds and casting stools. The photograph is a great panorama of an industrial site, illustrating a whole range of industrial buildings and equipment. There are a number of typical anonymous steel-clad structures serving all sorts of activities. Older brick buildings in the foreground house, amongst other services, a canteen. An overhead travelling crane in the near right corner spans and serves a scrap-yard and, weaving between the whole, there are a number of tightly curved railway lines. The large rearmost building, standing just left of centre, features two points of interest. Standing above the building and looking like stubby chimneys with cowls, are the two pig iron-smelting cupola furnaces. The building also has a common industrial space-saving feature, one that can be very useful to the modeller: its lower right corner has been cut back to allow a railway line to curve around it. The building is not cut back for its full height; the upper part of the building extends out over the line. One reason for doing this is to allow an overhead crane within to run the entire length of the building.

And, in the background, to the right of the cupolas and beyond the works itself, stands one of those then unremarkable, everyday gas-holders, which today are almost absent from our skylines.

An industrial panorama. This eclectic mix of buildings provides plenty of scope and inspiration for industrial modelling.
TATA STEEL EUROPE

A MODERN PROCESSING FACILITY

On a grey November day I photographed a view across Cargill's wheat-processing plant at Trafford Park, Manchester. Though railway lines, inset in concrete, are visible, they are no longer in use and are, in fact, truncated behind the photographer's position. Inevitably road vehicles feature, being the transport of choice today for many industrial concerns. The view shows a fairly modern industrial facility but in some ways it echoes some of the earlier dated photographs. Visible are concrete roadways, a patch of lawn, railway lines, pipework running hither and thither and small, functional brick buildings housing support services.

A modern processing facility. There is still plenty of scope for modelling heavy industry in a contemporary setting.

Grimy silos and intrusive vegetation. Older examples of industrial plant can present quite a challenge for weathering.

A modern power station. This gas-turbine power station is an essay in grey and stainless steel, which is very different in look to its predecessors.

GRIMY SILOS AND INTRUSIVE VEGETATION

Pesky vegetation creeps into the next photograph, which shows some ageing grain silos standing on the south bank of the Manchester Ship Canal in Trafford Park. I walked a couple of hundred yards alongside the canal on the Eccles side before finding a gap in the scrubby vegetation to obtain a view clear enough to photograph. Lichen and grime can be seen clinging to the sides of the silos and I believe that these have been standing here for many decades. At either side are seen the feed elevators and conveyor belt housings, and a dockside crane, with the yellow boom arm, sits right in front of the silos. It dips a suction hose into the holds of grain carriers on the canal to unload them.

A MODERN POWER STATION

Finally we have the gas-fired power station at Carrington, again on the south bank of the Manchester Ship Canal but a few miles further west. This stands on the site of the former coal-fired power station and, just off-shot to the left, stand the bridge and embankment that carry the former Cheshire Lines Committee railway. Again, this is a modern site without a railway connection but the photograph is included to show a very modern industrial facility with its shiny exhaust stacks and anonymous grey structures. There is nothing there that could not be modelled using techniques outlined in this book. For those not familiar with the Ship Canal, ships heading upstream did not have to navigate that weir! The canal has always functioned as a natural waterway with a flow downwards to the sea. Ships made their way through several sets of locks, while excess water flowed westwards over a number of weirs and spillways.

FINAL NOTES ON THE PROTOTYPE

Hopefully the preceding photographs have illustrated some points of interest and may even provide inspiration for some modelling. In subsequent chapters, to illustrate some features of the prototype, there will be references back to them. It really brings home just how much heavy industry the nation has lost when you go out and try to find examples. It is still there, not quite as grimy as it once was, and frequently difficult to photograph for reasons of security and visibility. Other prototype photographs feature in subsequent chapters where they feature structures on which the project builds are based.

CHAPTER THREE

TOOLS AND EQUIPMENT

In this chapter we'll look at the tools and equipment that have been used on the builds described in this volume.

A TOOL PHILOSOPHY

There are a number of maxims involving tools and I want to consider a couple of them before moving on to look at some of the tools themselves.

'Always use the right tool for the job' and 'only buy the best, they'll last a lifetime' are frequently suggested and, if money is no object, who could disagree? However, few of us have limitless resources, and budgets need to be balanced with priorities, investment with likely use. At the time of writing I heard a statistic quoted in the media claiming that most DIY electric drills sold see no more than ten minutes use in their lifetimes. If that is true, then the cheapest drill available would be adequate for most purchasers.

There is no doubt that the right tool makes the job both easier and quicker, that using the wrong tool can damage both the work piece and the tool, and can also present a risk of injury to the user. Having said that, many tasks can be completed using a fairly basic toolkit. Many specialist tools, and power tools in particular, merely speed up jobs that can be adequately performed with simpler and cheaper implements. Clearly, the using of a tool totally unsuited to a task is not recommended.

WORKSHOP SAFETY

I don't want to labour the safety issue. We're not using large machine tools or working in hazardous environments but it is worthwhile making a few observations. Always take a moment to *think about what you are about to do*; plan the job ahead, particularly with tasks you have not performed previously and especially if using power tools. Take care with knives and saws, and clamp the work piece firmly whenever possible. Wear eye protection if using power tools, make sure that the tools are properly fused and that the cables are in good condition. Some of the liquids we use are aggressive solvents, potentially toxic and are flammable. It's a good idea to decant such fluids into small bottles for immediate use, thereby minimizing the amount that can get spilled. Making a simple stand, or holding them firmly down with Blu-Tack, will considerably reduce the risk of knocking the bottle over in the first place. When using solvents, and always if spraying, ensure that there is a good flow of air around the work area. The safest place to spray paint, weather permitting, is outside. For indoor use, fairly inexpensive spray booths are available and are highly recommended if a lot of regular paint spraying is anticipated, as is the use of a decent face mask.

TOOLS AND WHERE TO BUY THEM

Basic modeller's tools are readily available from model shops, traders at exhibitions, tool merchants and by mail order from advertisements in the model press. These days a very convenient source of tools of all sorts is eBay, and you'll either be a fan and user of eBay or not. Either way, it is a useful resource to find what might be available, even if you buy elsewhere. By entering a vague tool description like 'circle cutter' or 'angle finder' into the search function, all sorts of options spring to view. Living in a rural area, the ability to buy some unusual tool or fitting and have it delivered to my door is, to me, invaluable. Mention should be made here of the two German budget supermarkets, Aldi and Lidl. They run 'specials', often themed, and these regularly include tools. Over the years they've provided me with all sorts of useful bits, including needle files, small screwdrivers, clamps, multi-drawer storage units, pull saws and mini-drills. They usually cost just two or three pounds, rarely more than ten pounds, and are of good quality. The difficulty is that these ranges run until they sell out so you need to keep an eye on their respective websites to see what is coming up. Most items seem to reappear in subsequent promotions.

Tools generally make tasks easier, quicker and the result more accurate. Many tasks can be performed without them. There is clearly no point buying an expensive and highly specialized tool to be used just the once. Some tools are pretty much essential and it would be near impossible to model without them. Those covered in the basic modeller's tool section will be in this category and they will largely be those tools already in any modeller's toolkit.

Later we'll cover some more specialized tools. Few of them, if any, should be considered indispensable and some are costly. Their use can speed up certain tasks and, if they are likely to see regular use,

the cost may be justified by the time they save. Some of them have uses beyond the modelling bench for general DIY jobs and household repairs.

THE BASIC MODELLER'S TOOLKIT

The focus here is on tools used to work with styrene, card and foamboard, and with which to build structures. There would be a different emphasis for a toolkit to build an etched locomotive kit, for example. A steel rule and a decent craft knife are clearly must-haves. They were used extensively in every project in this book and indeed you could, with determination, build many things using little else.

MEASURING AND MARKING

Considering the basic tools in groups we might start with measuring and marking-out tools. A steel ruler is essential, both for measuring and for use as a straight edge when cutting. A 12in/300mm ruler is the most useful size but there are occasions when a shorter rule is useful and, when building structures on the size described later, longer lengths are helpful. I have 24in/600mm and 36in/900mm rulers. Set squares,

A selection of rulers, squares, protractors and gauges used to measure, to mark angles and to provide cutting edges for craft knives.

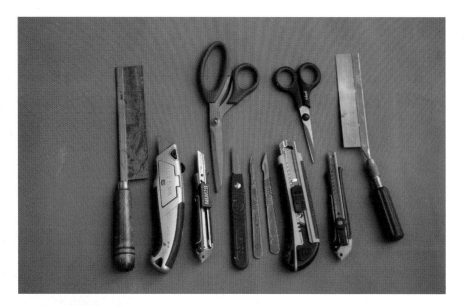

Some of the many scalpels, craft knives, razor saws and scissors I've acquired over the years.

again of different sizes, are essential and a device for measuring and setting-out angles will be very useful. Some decent sharp pencils, a fine permanent marker pen and a scriber or two are required to mark out measurements and cutting lines.

CUTTING

For cutting, knives with replacement blades are the most useful. A Swann Morton scalpel, a couple of 'snap-off' knives with 9mm and 18mm blades, and a heavy duty Stanley knife type, will all cover all needs. A razor saw with a suitable mitre block will take care of heavier cutting duties. Scissors, in different sizes, are useful to have to hand.

SHAPING AND CLEANING UP

A set of needle files can be useful, though they are best suited to metal working and they soon clog with use on plastics and the like. Larger, coarser files are often more effective and, in both cases, older and cheaper versions are worth keeping aside for structure modelling. Cosmetic nail files, available from chemist's shops and Boots, are a cheap and effective method of filing the types of materials commonly used in building construction. A selection of sand and emery papers in various grades is very useful and it is worth making sanding pads in various sizes by sticking emery paper on to squares and rectangles of

thin MDF. I use PVA white glue to make them up and leave them overnight under a stack of books to dry. They are very useful for quickly removing material and truing up edges and corners.

I keep a small palm sander handy for the occasional task, thinning the edges on Wills building sheets, for example. I also have a Minicraft disc sander, which is useful for cleaning up the ends on larger plastic sections.

DRILLS

For drilling holes, a pin vice and a selection of small drill bits are basic essentials. Cheap sets containing a large number of bits in a wide range of sizes are available, and though their quality and accuracy might horrify an engineer, for structure modelling in plastic they are usually good enough. They can be a useful starter set while a set of higher quality bits is collected. An Archimedean drill, rotated by sliding the collar down the spiral body, can be useful as can a modeller's power drill, of which a wide range is available. I have found a rechargeable modeller's drill by Dremel useful for structure modelling, though I rarely used it when I was building etched locomotive kits. A modeller's drill will often come as a set that will include a number of grinding burrs and sanding drums, and these are quite useful at times. For larger holes, a cheap DIY-sized rechargeable drill and some

Tools for sanding and shaping. The homemade sanding sticks being the most useful when modelling buildings.

Various drilling tools: hand-powered, low-voltage, cordless and mains voltage.

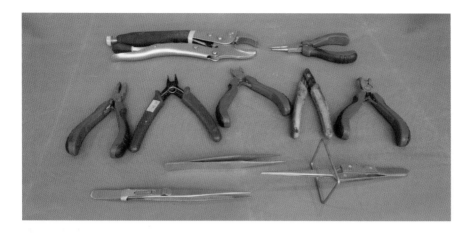

Tweezers are an essential modeller's tool. Reasonable pliers and cutting tools can be bought fairly cheaply though the Xuron range is worth their extra cost.

appropriate bits can be very useful and obviously has wider applications around the house.

HOLDING, GRIPPING AND CROPPING

Tweezers have an obvious place in the toolkit and I have several pairs, including some that can be locked on the work piece. I also have a pair of tweezers that have a small, square metal stand built into them. This allows them to sit on the workbench whilst holding an object. They can be seen in the right foreground of the photograph above, showing tweezers. A selection of small pliers of different types will find many uses:

conventional, needle-nosed, curved and flat-jawed. A selection of small side- and end-cutters is equally useful. Good-quality cutters are needed for metal and those by Xuron, though not cheap, are highly recommended. For cutting plastic, cheap ones are more than adequate. A small modeller's vice is a 'nice to have', though I rarely use mine when engaged in structure modelling; it sees far more use when building etched kits.

CLAMPING

I frequently use clamps and grips to hold items while glue is setting. Where I want really strong bonds,

None of these clamps were expensive but they do the job.

I'll leave them overnight either clamped together directly or between two bits of wood, if that is appropriate. Perfectly useable clamps are available quite cheaply and if I'm working on a large project, or several smaller projects at the same time, I can have a dozen in use at one time.

SPECIALIZED TOOLS

The tools looked at now are those that are less likely to be found in a basic modeller's toolbox, tools that might have limited applications but will speed up certain tasks and make repetitive work so much easier. Some will be well suited to working with larger objects than the small-scale modeller normally encounters. A couple of the tools are homemade and some are not cheap. Whether or not they can be justified will be determined by how much use they will see and how much time they will save, something only the individual can decide.

CIRCLE CUTTERS

I use one or other of these very often for cutting discs or round holes in styrene and foamboard. Cutting in styrene is easy enough, but for foamboard I usually drill through the board at the desired centre and then use a cutter to cut through the card surface on either side. The cut through the foam is completed using a scalpel and following the lines cut into the surface.

Occasionally I need to draw or cut a circle that is larger than any of the commercially available tools will manage. The cooling pond, which sits under the cooling tower described in Chapter 11, is an example of the need to cut out a large circle. I struggled to find anything large enough until I found some trammel points. These clamp to a bar (I use 12mm square brass) and can be used with a pencil to draw a circle. I soldered a nut to one end of the bar and can clamp a large Swann Morton scalpel blade to it. Cutting styrene with it is straightforward but care needs to

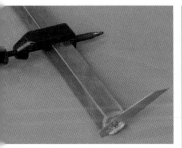

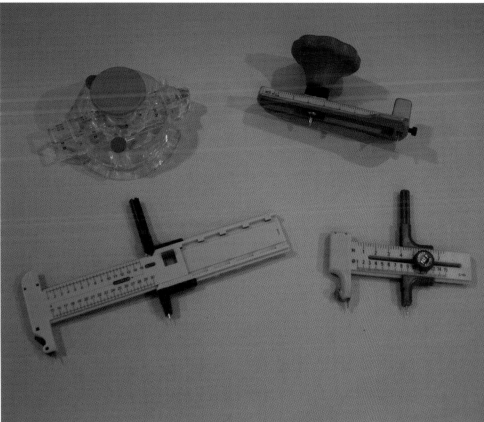

ABOVE: *My home-assembled trammel cutter for large circles. It comprises a commercial trammel point clamped to a length of brass section. A Swann Morton scalpel blade can be clamped onto the end.*

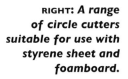

RIGHT: *A range of circle cutters suitable for use with styrene sheet and foamboard.*

be taken when cutting 10mm foamboard. If the blade attempts to cut too deeply, it drags and distorts the cut. It takes a little practice to rotate the cutter bar without allowing the blade to dig in too deeply.

HOLE AND DISC PUNCHES, AND HOLE-ENLARGERS

A leather punch will very quickly produce discs of styrene in a range of small sizes, so is a very useful tool to have handy. Umbrella-type hole-enlargers, used at low speed in a cordless drill, are useful for opening-out larger holes in a styrene sheet. They are also used to ream out the ends of plastic tubing to give the impression of a thin wall, e.g. the top of a steel chimney.

JEWELLER'S DISC PUNCHES AND DOMING TOOL

These are not cheap; the larger disc punch cost around £80 if I recall correctly. They are designed for the punching of discs from thin sheet metal and work equally well for punching styrene. The method of use is probably clear from the photographs. The sheet is placed under the appropriate-sized hole and, using the appropriate machined punch and a hammer, the disc is cut out. They are not only useful for punching discs but also producing round holes. By careful alignment, it is possible to produce rings of styrene too. On the larger punch, the top plate can be clamped down on to the sheet prior to punching. By then using the hole-enlargers mentioned above, holes of pretty much any size can be produced. The doming tool's function is also fairly obvious. It is used to turn flat discs of soft metals into 'cups' or domes. Not used regularly but handy enough on occasions. These are perfect examples of tools that can only be justified if they are to be used extensively. I use the disc punches frequently.

CENTRE FINDER

This simple little device, illustrated with a styrene disc, enables the centre of a disc to be located and marked.

MITRE CHOPPERS

Two of the most widely used specialized tools are the two cutters or choppers featured in the accompanying photograph. Both do pretty much the same job, cutting

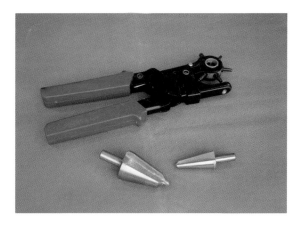

A simple leather punch will quickly produce small discs of styrene. The 'umbrella'-style hole-enlargers enable any size of larger hole to be produced.

Jeweller's tools, two disc punches and a doming block. Specialized, not particularly cheap but they are very useful tools nonetheless.

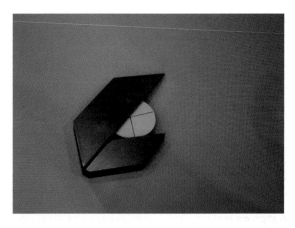

The tool for finding the centre of a circle or disc.

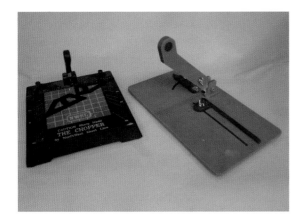

Mitre 'choppers' for use with styrene. The NWSL Chopper II on the left and the Proses' version on the right. Though similar, each has its own advantages.

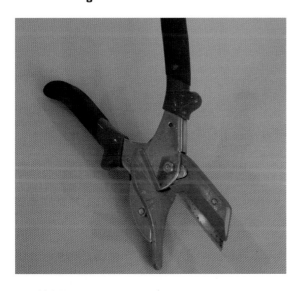

A hand-held 'chopper' useful for quick, non-repetitive, cutting of styrene sections.

A styrene scriber used for marking joint lines on styrene.

styrene to length and at pre-set angles and, by setting the guides, accurate, repetitive cuts can be made. A real time-saver, e.g. when cutting the ribs for the gas-holder. The NWSL Chopper is made in the US and uses single-edge razor blades. The more recent Proses Cutter is made in Turkey and Bachmann are now the distributors. It uses two lengths of 9mm 'snap-off' type cutting blades. I believe that a later version with a more comprehensive set of guides is now available.

HAND SHEARS

I bought this having seen one used on a YouTube modelling demonstration. A couple of designs are available: one has a fixed blade, mine has a replacement Stanley knife type blade, and I have seen one recently that incorporates an angle-cutting guide. It's quick and easy to use for occasional square and angle cuts on styrene sections.

SCRIBER

A craft knife can be used to scribe lines on styrene to represent joints between panels and sections. A cut with a blade can be a bit narrow and a scriber like this one, run along the cut, removes a little 'V' of plastic and gives a better effect.

PIPE CUTTERS

For scribing around plastic tube to form panel joints for pipework, steel chimneys or storage tanks, I use pipe cutters. I have three that cover a wide range

Pipe cutters in various sizes and a large jubilee clip, used for scribing seams around pipe.

of diameters and they are a very quick, accurate and effective method for scribing lines on plastic tubing. They are less useful for cutting plastic tube; the material can tend to flatten out if too much pressure is applied to the cutter blade. A cheaper alternative is to use a jubilee clip as a scribing guide. One was used to scribe the 75mm pipe used in the tank farm project.

SAWS AND MITRE BLOCKS

Mention has already been made of standard razor saws and mitre blocks, but for larger jobs. I also have a range of fine-toothed pull saws. The two-bladed one was obtained from Lidl. They make short work of cutting through plastic tube and resin, giving a very fine finish. The clamping mitre block is a very handy aid to use with them.

MITRE SAWS

A hand mitre saw in a frame is handy too, especially for cutting wood and MDF. I sometimes resort to a workshop-sized power mitre saw for cutting large items such as heavy walled pipe. A recent acquisition was a Proxxon powered mitre saw. Proxxon power tools are of very high quality, but that comes at a price. With its accurate clamping mechanism, it speeds up the process of producing angled cuts, e.g. when making a gusseted bend in pipework.

FOAMWERK'S CUTTERS

I came across these specialist tools on eBay. Made by Logan, in the USA, they are designed for working with foamboard. Essentially they are customized handles into which a special blade is clamped, and by drawing the tool across the surface, the foamboard is cut. The blades can be clamped at different depths to either cut through or score into the board. Each tool is designed for a different cut along a straight edge, one at 90 degrees and another at 45 degrees. Another tool cuts a rebate along an edge for joining two sheets and yet another is designed for free-form cutting. The two larger tools are designed to slide

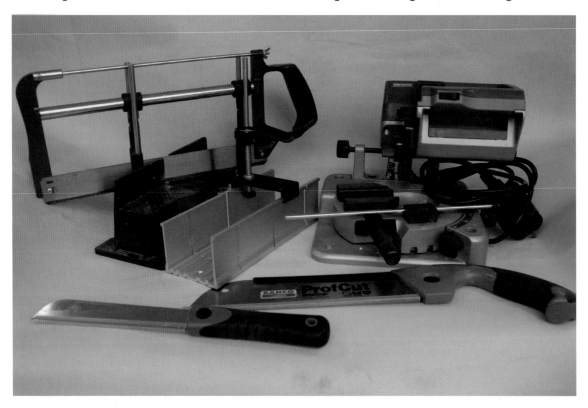

Larger saws, two 'pull' saws for fine cuts, a clamping mitre saw block and the Proxxon chop saw.

Foamwerks' cutters from left to right, straight cutter, rebate cutter and angle cutter. At the rear, the guided cutters; left, 'V' cutter; and, right, the straight cutter along with the guide.

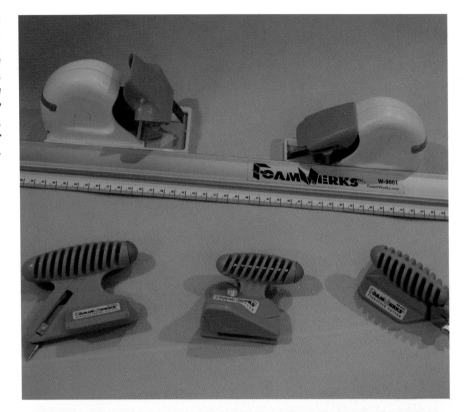

Foamwerks. The insect-like cutters are designed to slide along the Foamwerks' straight edge. The straight cutter is particularly useful if large amounts of foamboard are to be cut.

An office guillotine.

along Foamwerk's own straight-edge cutting guide: one cuts at 90 degrees, the other cuts a 'V' groove. They are by no means essential tools, just helpful if you are working with a lot of foamboard. The one I use the most is the larger 90-degree cutter, along with the cutter guide. There is also a circular cutter in the range but it seems to have no advantage over cutters I already have.

GUILLOTINE

I bought this thinking that it might be a good way of cutting lengths of narrow strip from styrene sheet but found it was rather difficult to keep the cuts parallel to the edge, though it works well enough with thin card.

ADHESIVES

Four main adhesives are used in the majority of these projects. If it is anticipated that these adhesives will be used extensively, it may be cost-efficient to buy them in larger sizes than commonly sold to the modeller. Conversely, there is no benefit in buying too much, just to lie in storage for months or even years, as some of them do not keep well.

White wood glue or PVA is the best adhesive for use with foamboard, MDF and any other wood. With foamboard it sticks both the card and the foam without damaging the latter. Usually I apply it and then hold the components in place with masking tape, clamps or, if appropriate, under weighted boards. Within an hour so it forms a reasonable bond but is best left overnight to develop full strength. I buy 5ltr containers and decant into smaller dispensers for use on the workbench. It is best applied using a brush of suitable size for the task in hand. For sticking large surface areas or applying groundcover, I may dilute it with, perhaps, 25 per cent water.

For sticking plastic sheet to foamboard, or any other dissimilar materials together, and where there

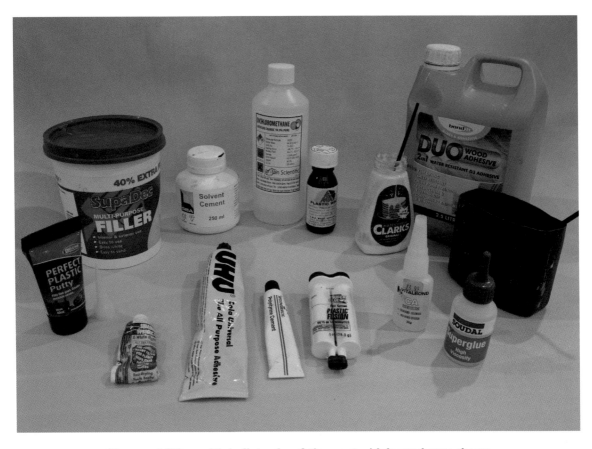

Glues and fillers with bulk packs of the most widely used ones shown.
Smaller containers for use on the workbench stand alongside.

is a reasonable surface area, I use UHU clear adhesive. It is clear and soon forms a strong bond. It does tend to string, so needs to be applied carefully. I don't use traditional Evo-Stick with plastic sheet. It continues to give off solvent fumes for weeks after initial use and these fumes can soften and wrinkle the plastic.

For styrene, and most other modeller's plastics, the adhesive most widely used is probably MekPak. It is water-like in nature and needs to be brushed on using a small paint brush. Another widely used modeller's solvent is Plastic Weld. Both can be bought much more economically in bulk by their chemical names butanone and dichloromethane, respectively. Bearing in mind that both of these are very aggressive solvents, and are highly flammable, if the option of buying in bulk is chosen, then they should be carefully and safely stored. As they are both volatile liquids they readily evaporate, so keep the bottles tightly

capped. Buying very large volumes, amounts that will not be used within a few months at the most, may not be economical as they may just evaporate away.

As I use a fair amount of this type of solvent I buy dichloromethane via eBay in either 500ml or 1,000ml plastic containers. It is recommended that it should be decanted into a glass bottle at the first opportunity. Most importantly, the bulk container should not be used as the workshop dispenser. The health and safety hazards of knocking over and spilling half a litre or more of this type of solvent on the workbench does not bear thinking about. I have a number of old Plastic Weld bottles that I keep for this purpose and I only fill those by about a third for use on my workbench. As they retain their original labels, I also know exactly what is in them.

Cyanoacrylate or superglue is the fourth adhesive that I use regularly. I buy 50ml containers of medium

Tints for paint. Available in wide range of colours they are ideal for colouring emulsions and masonry paints.

viscosity superglue and use it for fixing small components and for bonds where there is little surface area.

Four other adhesives see occasional use. Araldite is used where gap filling is required and between dissimilar materials. I use polystyrene cement in tubes for cementing large areas of styrene, particularly sheet, together. The MekPak and Plastic Weld solvents evaporate very rapidly and it can be difficult to get enough 'wet' solvent quickly enough onto a large area. Cement from a tube overcomes this problem. Plastic Fusion is an adhesive that I came across on a modelling 'How to' video on YouTube. It is a two-part epoxy resin specially formulated for use with a wide range of plastics. It has an Araldite-like consistency and is best suited for gap filling in larger joints. I use it to strengthen joints between the type of plastic used for plumbing pipe, which does not always respond well to conventional modelling glues. Finally there is plumber's solvent for use with those plastics used to make plumbing and drainage pipe.

FILLERS

For gap filling between styrene components I use Perfect Plastic Putty from DeLuxe Materials or Squadron White filler, both designed for use with plastics. As a general filler for larger volumes, particularly with wood or on scenic boards, a water-based DIY-type filler is cheap and easy to use. They can be let down with a little water and applied with a brush if that suits the job in hand. Plastic Padding epoxy filler finds occasional use as it sets very quickly and strongly. All of these fillers can be readily carved or sanded once dry.

ADHESIVE TAPES

Various types of tape always come in handy for masking or holding items together. Duct or Gaffa tape, double-sided adhesive tape, PVC tape and various masking tapes are regularly used during my

Adhesive tapes with the narrow 'pinstriping' tapes at the front.

project builds. Masking tape, once painted, makes a decent representation of flashing around roofing details. I also use very narrow, down to 0.5mm, pre-cut masking tape to represent detail on ridge tiles, gutters and downpipes and so on.

SOLDERING

Considered by many modellers to be somewhat of a dark art, it may come as a relief for some to know that soldering plays almost no part, at least, no essential part, in these projects. Soldering was used to butt join the end of a brass rod to

another rod on the gas-holder, and the etched caged ladders and the 'steel' water tank were also assembled using solder. In all of these cases non-soldered alternatives were available, either superglue with the brass components or the use of plastic components in the first place.

Consequently we will not spend any time on soldering other than to say that nevertheless it is a very useful skill for the modeller to acquire and it can be readily learned. There are many tutorials in print and online to give guidance but, in the end, you need to fire up the soldering iron and practice with some bits of scrap brass.

CHAPTER FOUR

MATERIALS AND PAINTING

The two main structural materials that I use are foamboard and various forms of polystyrene plastic, sheet and sections. I also use some thin MDF sheet.

FOAMBOARD

Foamboard is widely used in the advertising industry to make display boards. It consists of a layer of expanded foam sandwiched between two layers of thin card, or sometimes plastic, and is available in various thicknesses, 2, 3, 4, 5, 6, 8, 10, 13 and 19mm. The plastic-coated sheet doesn't glue so well and has, for the modeller, no particular advantage. Most foamboard seems to have an expanded polystyrene core, the white bubbly material used in packaging. This is okay as it cuts well enough but the foam will dissolve if it comes into contact with some glues and paints. I prefer a board filled with a polyurethane foam. This type of foam has a greater density, is a creamy colour and cuts much more cleanly. It is also resistant to some of the glues and solvents that modeller's commonly use. It does not dissolve when coming into contact with Plastic Weld or car-type aerosol paints. The brand I use is made in Germany and is sold as Foam-X. Foamboards can be bought from some craft and art suppliers, from online retailers and through eBay; the polyurethane foam sheets may need a little tracking down from specialist suppliers. Sheet sizes range from A4 up to 2,440 x 1,220mm (8 x 4ft). Generally the 5 and 10mm thicknesses, and in A4 or A3 sizes, cover most needs, though for very large structures the larger sheets are very useful. I tend to buy larger sizes, though it should be borne in mind that they take up quite a bit of storage space and can be cumbersome when they are being cut. Foamboard is light, very easy to cut, stable and fully self-supporting. The best adhesive to use is PVA, white glue, which will not attack the foam and will stick both the foam and the card. For gluing materials other than card to foamboard, UHU is a suitable choice of adhesive.

If, in the final build, the foamboard will be an internal carcass and therefore unseen, the the exposed foam edges are not a problem. However, if cut edges will be seen, then the exposed foam needs to be covered. I use 250gsm white card bought in A3 sheets. Cut into 5 or 10mm strips, as appropriate, these are glued with PVA along the exposed edge, providing a finished look that can be painted or textured.

Though its plain white surface could be painted to represent some finishes, its main use is a structural material to build a carcass, which is then clad in an appropriate printed paper or textured styrene sheet.

STYRENE

Styrene sheet and sections have long been modeller's staples. Sheet is available plain or embossed with a number of surface effects. The best-known UK supplier is Slater's. Wills provide an alternative range of textured plastic building sheets, though these are much thicker and come in smaller sizes.

Lengths of styrene are available in a wide range of end sections; flat bar, thin strips, square, 'I', 'C', 'H' girders and solid and hollow rounds in a wide range of sizes. They are available from a number of suppliers. I use a lot of both Evergreen sections and Plastruct components. The Plastruct range includes truss girders, caged ladders, stairways and handrails. There are also suppliers based in China selling styrene sections on eBay and although relatively inexpensive, they are not quite of the Evergreen quality. One drawback is that they are sold in packs containing an assortment of specified sections but you cannot buy them in packs of one size and shape.

The solid sections, round and square, and round tube, are of a very usable quality and I have a number of assorted packs lying by my workbench. The channel sections are okay but less crisply extruded than are those from the established suppliers.

CORRUGATED IRON SHEETING

Actually corrugated steel, this was once a very widely used material to clad industrial structures. There is still plenty of it around, though it has largely been superseded by more modern coated, and often insulated, profiled steel sheeting. There are a number of options available to the modeller, particularly in 4mm scale, to represent it. Vacuum-formed sheet has somewhat oversized corrugations and is not used in any of the projects covered. Thin, corrugated metal foil is also available. It can look very good but for large structures can be costly and slow to work with.

WILLS CORRUGATED IRON SHEET

Wills offer a moulded corrugated sheet in their range and in common with the other types it is thick enough to be self-supporting on small structures but at the cost of being more difficult to cut. The sheets are also small, so several are required for larger buildings and this brings about the necessity of joining them. Larger buildings also negate the self-supporting advantage of the sheets; joining several sheets edge on is not ideal strength-wise and a substructure will be required. The need for joining sheets also raises another of their drawbacks: making invisible joins between sheets vertically is challenging and horizontally virtually impossible. With careful cutting and finishing, and then pushing the sheets very firmly together with plenty of solvent, a reasonable vertical joint is possible. However, horizontal joints are very, very difficult. The horizontal rows of sheet are purposely moulded in a rustic irregular pattern that is impossible to match between sheets, and the sheet itself contains 2½ rows.

Stacking these sheets one above the other results in a strange and non-prototypical arrangement of full and half-length rows. Cutting off the half-row doesn't help: not only is it wasteful but the irregular level is impossible to match up. The irregular rustic laying of sheets

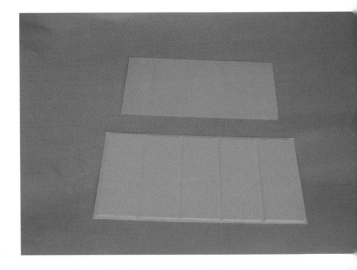

Vacuum-formed and moulded corrugated sheeting.

portrayed in the moulding may be fine for a building knocked up by a farmer or small business, but it is problematic for large industrial buildings. These buildings would have been built by professional steel erectors who would have taken care and pride in the neat and regular laying of individual sheets. The odd one might slip later as fittings corrode but essentially each row of sheets would be level. Having said all that, Wills sheets can be used to make a more rustic structure and, with care, can pass muster on even large buildings.

I used Wills sheets on the Pomona building, featured in Chapter 16, and a ruse used here was to mask as many of the horizontal lines as possible with pipework, walkways and windows. As a method it works well enough but limits the ability to model large, blank building sides.

CORRUGATED STYRENE SHEET

This widely available material offers a number of advantages: it is easy to cut and shape, easy to glue, cost-effective on large structures and can be joined near invisibly. It is not actually corrugated; rather it has a series of fine ribs moulded on to one side giving a corrugated effect. It is available from several manufacturers and though individual sheets look fine, the slight variations in the pitch of the corrugations can cause minor mismatches if used together. It's worth obtaining all the sheets for a single project at one time.

PREPARING THE SHEETS

Prototype sheets of corrugated steel seem to have been most commonly 8ft tall and in widths of 2, 3 and 4ft. The styrene sheets require a little preparation before use. The first task is to replicate the vertical joints between individual sheets. Decide on your chosen sheet width and measure this, to scale, across the sheet. Count the number of corrugations which that covers and mark out the panels by counting the ribs. With Slater's 4mm corrugated sheet I use a spacing of ten corrugations.

Using a steel rule and a scalpel, take care, and lightly score down each marked groove the full length of the sheet. The aim is to raise a slight lip so that an effect of overlapping sheets is produced. I start with a very light, near vertical, scribe to make a guide cut. This is followed by two equally light scribes but with the scalpel held at a shallow angle, cutting into the side of the corrugation. Inevitably, some cuts will go all the way through but this should be minimized. It is not a major problem – you will just end up with shorter lengths of sheeting after the next step, which is to cut the sheet into horizontal strips.

Mark off down the side of the corrugated styrene sheet the height of each individual sheet required: 32mm for an 8ft sheet in 4mm. I actually cut them

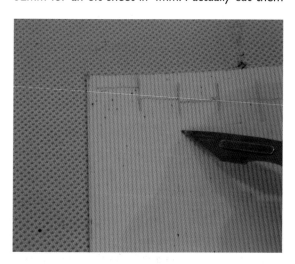

Slater's corrugated sheeting, marked for width and showing the method of scoring the vertical joints in order to raise a lip.

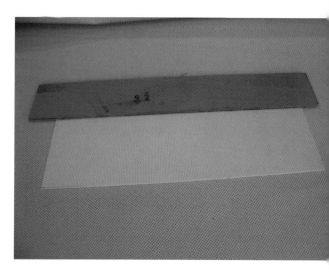

The 40mm steel bar used to cut the sheets into individual rows.

out 40mm deep and have a length of 40mm steel strip, which enables me to very quickly reduce an A4 sheet into strips. An alternative is to use a large steel square against the edge and then cut horizontally right through the sheet, using two passes if necessary, so several strips of corrugated panelling are produced. At this point I gently roll the sheet round to help open up the scribed 'joint lines'.

Having prepared the styrene sheet, take the foamboard carcass of the building to be clad and draw a line horizontally to mark the lowest edge of the cladding. Using that as a baseline, mark further horizontal lines, carrying them across any doorways or other openings right up to the top edge. Set these lines at a spacing that will give a 5mm overlap with your chosen sheet depth. As my sheets are cut 40mm deep, I set the spacing at 35mm.

THE BASIC CLADDING PROCEDURE

Cladding starts at the bottom by fitting the lowest row of sheets and then moving upwards one row at a time. If, as is usually the case, there is a dwarf brick wall at the bottom of the wall, and this has been made using styrene brickwork, then the lower edge of the cladding can be overlapped on the upper edge of the brickwork. If brickpaper has been used, or

Cladding continued level across an opening.

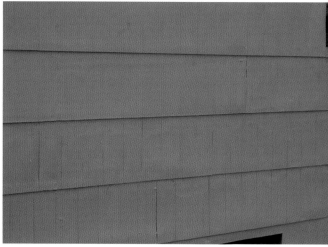

An area clad and awaiting painting.

there is no dwarf wall at all, I start by gluing a narrow strip of 20 thou styrene along the lower edge.

Starting from the left, attach lengths of the prepared cladding strips so that they sit on the lower strip with the upper edge on the marked line. Solvent is used to stick them to the lower strip of styrene, and contact adhesive to adhere them, at the upper edge, to the foamboard. Add the next strip of corrugated panels to the right. Fix in the same manner with the addition of solvent to make the butt joint between adjacent strips. This joint does not need to be fully disguised, but it needs to give the appearance of a joint between two sheets of corrugated iron. It helps to sand a small bevel on the edge of the sheet being added such that it snuggles just a little under the edge of the strip to which it is being joined. The joint will look little different from the scribed 'false' joints. At doorway edges or corners leave an overlap of 10mm or so and cut them back in a straight line when the whole aperture has been clad around.

Complete a single horizontal row then start on the next row up. This row is added in just the same manner with the lower edge overlapping the top of the row below. I try to keep the scribed vertical joints aligned, though after laying a horizontal strip or two they seem to drift. I trim back the strip a little to get them back in line. To complete the process, carry on until the entire wall is clad, cutting back the top

row at eaves' level, as required. It is worth staggering the joints between strips to help disguise them further and this also strengthens the cladding. The horizontal overlaps are apparent straightaway; the scribed, vertical 'overlaps' will become more visible once painted and weathered. The photographs will, I trust, make this process clear. With a little practice, a large building can be clad surprisingly quickly. This process was used on all of the larger structures on the Staplegrove module and on the open-hearth melting shop featured in Chapter 14.

WILLS CORRUGATED ASBESTOS SHEETING

No longer made or used owing to the health hazard the fibres pose, asbestos cement sheeting was once a very widely used cladding medium for industrial structures. Perhaps not so common as corrugated steel sheeting, it was nonetheless seen in many environments, even on steelworks' buildings. It does not corrode and other advantages include longevity, fire resistance, and a degree of heat and sound insulation.

Having expressed reservations about the use of Wills corrugated iron sheeting, Wills corrugated asbestos sheeting is in a different league altogether. Yes, it is thick, which presents some difficulty in cutting, but the moulding is excellent and the panels represent two full rows of sheets, nicely aligned, which makes joining sheets very easy. The edges should be cleaned up first with a sanding stick. Using plenty of solvent brushed between them to soften the plastic, if they are pushed firmly together, virtually invisible joints can be achieved.

If the edge of the sheet will be visible, e.g. along the eaves of a roof, it will benefit from being thinned down. Abrasive paper stuck to a piece of MDF works well or using a small power sander will considerably speed up the process. Once thinned, it can be further improved by filing matching corrugations on the underside with a round needle file. This method is suggested on the Wills packaging.

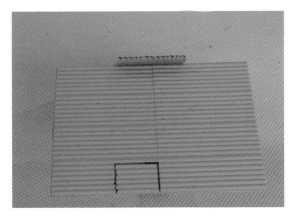

Wills corrugated asbestos sheeting showing an 'improved edge'.

BRICKWORK

I've used both printed brickpapers and brick-embossed styrene sheet on the projects described here. I download brickpapers from the Scalescenes' website. You choose the type of brick you want, pay a single fee to download the PDF and then print copies whenever you need them. The embossed brickwork styrene I use is Slater's and is available in different patterns or bonds. It has a degree of structural strength and small bits can be used unsupported, though generally I back it with 40 thou styrene on small structures and foamboard on larger ones. I usually pre-paint and give a degree of weathering to embossed brickwork whilst it is still a flat sheet.

Pre-painted and weathered brick-effect styrene sheet. Further weathering is applied once the finished building is in place.

CONCRETE

To replicate the appearance of concrete, I mostly use suede-effect paint from PlastiKote. It dries with a slightly gritty texture and the tan colour gives a reasonable representation of established concrete. An alternative for flat surfaces, roofs and roadways, for example, is to use a fine, 240 grit abrasive paper and paint it with thin coats. Precision Paints sell a couple of 'grey' concrete colours and Tamiya Buff acrylic gives the browner look of older concrete. I haven't used them but concrete-effect sheets are available from Scalescenes.

Concrete effects: 240-grit emery paper sprayed with 'Suede' effect paint with pots of Precision Paints Concrete, Tamiya 'Buff' and a can of Plastikote 'Suede'.

WINDOWS

All of the windows installed on the projects in this book are of the metal-framed type. Crittal is the best-known manufacturer of the real windows, though there were, and are, others. Such multi-paned windows have been almost standard fittings for industrial use for many years. Being steel, often galvanized, they do not rot and last for years.

I have modelled them in three different ways. On the gas-holder described in Chapter 6, the frames were simply drawn on to clear sheet using paint and a bowpen; from a distance they look fine. On the small, hoist building at the base of the gas-holder and on the rear extension of the canteen building the frames were made up with strips of styrene applied to the clear sheet. This is a slow process, though, with care, frames of any type can be made up.

My preference is to use etched brass frames. Some types and sizes are available commercially and I have used the grid-pattern frames available from Scalelink on the coal-blending plant and tank farm pumphouse. I subsequently ventured into the world of custom etching and had some frames produced to match those on the prototype roll shop shown in Chapter 10, along with some other frames for other projects. I was very pleased with the result and will use this method again. Brass window frames have the advantage that they can be used as their own template for cutting the correct-sized opening in the styrene building walls.

Whatever the source of the etches, the production of the completed window unit is the same. After cutting the frames from the main etch and cleaning them up, they are primed with an aerosol and then painted, either by hand or with an airbrush. Most are finished in the washed-out pale green that is the standard for my fictional steel company and for many real indus-trial concerns. These are left to dry for a day at least. The backs of the frames are then sprayed with Display Mount adhesive and the frames stuck down onto a sheet of 15 thou clear glazing material. A piece of clear polythene, just cut from a plastic bag, is laid on top of the frames, followed by a flat board and either weights or clamps. The polythene prevents the frames stick-ing to the board while the glue sets. Again, the frames are left overnight and the following day, using a new scalpel blade, the individual glazed frames are cut from the clear sheet. They are fixed in place using either, or often both, superglue or Johnson's Klear floor polish. For some years Klear has been used by modeller's to fix and even improve the appearance of plastic glazing materials. The original, and now unavailable, formulation was a water-like liquid that could be brushed on; it dries hard and clear. I have a couple of bottles that will last me years. The current formulation is not a clear liquid but I believe that it dries clear and otherwise gives the same results, though I haven't used it.

Etched window-frames from Scalelink, with my own pattern etched fret at the front.

Etched window-frames having the glazing material affixed. The etch and glazing are glued and then clamped between layers of polythene and foamboard.

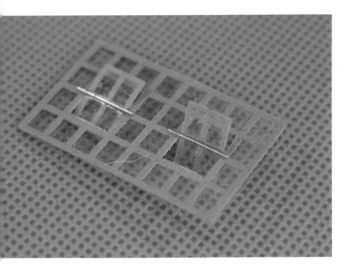

My method of representing the hinged window on an etched window-frame fret.

I had some of the windows etched with an opening and a matching small frame. On the prototypes these are hinged across their centres and can be rotated horizontally to open them. I superglue a small length of brass wire across the centre and fix them in an open position.

PAINTING AND FINISHING

Painting can make or break a model. It is the surface that we see and on the model must replicate the surface finish of the prototype, which might be paint or it might be brick, concrete, tarmac, water and so on.

PREPARATION

Once I am happy that the surface is finished, i.e. cleaned and free from blemishes and dog hairs, I almost universally use acrylic car primer aerosol paint as the first coat on any model I build. Usually grey, but occasionally red oxide if that better suits the planned finish. Easy to obtain, these aerosol paints are simple to apply, help mask small blemishes, yet show up anything requiring some remedial work. They are safe to use on card, plastic and metal but they do need to be used where plenty of ventilation is available – outdoors preferably. Less so with building construction, but sometimes when finishing locomotive kits, the use of a white primer

undercoat is helpful if the topcoat is going to be yellow. Yellow paint has quite a poor opacity and the undercoat will show through unless a very heavy topcoat is used.

FINISHING COATS

For large areas or complex, intricate shapes my first choice is generally an aerosol spray for speed and convenience. A huge range of such paints is available; enamels and acrylics from the traditional modelling suppliers like Humbrol and Tamiya. One I use frequently is Humbrol Gunmetal spray as a base coat for anything made of steel. The range of colours available from the various aerosol car paint suppliers is vast. They are gloss and may be a little heavy at times, but are worth considering for many applications. Many other ranges of aerosol paints of different formulations and colours can also be sourced from DIY stores.

SPECIALITY PAINTS

One range I use is the Montana range. These paints are the spray of choice for the graffiti artist, which may not endear them to you, nonetheless they are a useful resource. They take a little getting used to as they work at a lower pressure than other aerosols and the paint is applied quite thickly. They are no use for fine finishes, e.g. smaller scale locomotives and rolling stock, but on larger constructions can be very useful. They are available in gloss and matt finishes with a wide range of colours and are very hard-wearing. Many of the colours are pastels or are very bright and have little utility for the modeller, but I have found plenty of more muted colours suitable for industrial structures and even G scale rolling-stock. The blue and green buildings on the Staplegrove module were finished with Montana matt sprays and a gloss Greenblack was used as the base water colour for the cooling tower and water tanks.

TEXTURED PAINTS

A search of the shelves in DIY and craft stores will reveal a number of aerosol paints for specialist applications and finishes. A very useful aerosol paint is Plasticotes' Suede finish. It seemed to disappear from

A selection of aerosol paints, automotive primers, some examples from the Montana range and Plastikotes 'Suede' effect sprays.

the shelves for a couple of years but, at the end of 2016, was available again. Suede paint is available in three colours – sand and two shades of brown – but its main attribute is that it gives a slightly coarse, gritty finish, ideal for replicating concrete or as a starting point for a rusty texture. It was used on a few of the projects in this volume, e.g. the concrete water-tower, the concrete footings for the overhead crane and the cooling tower. The sand colour gives an aged-concrete look – concrete that has lost its initial cement whiteness.

There are other aerosols giving even coarser finishes, though I have yet to find a modelling use for them.

BASIC PAINTS

I use a wide a range of the usual modeller's paints, Humbrol enamels and Tamiya acrylics largely, but like many modellers, I have all sorts of others obtained over the years. I buy thinners in 5ltr containers, white spirit for enamels and isopropyl alcohol for acrylics.

Re-cycled squeezy bottles, isopropyl alcohol on the left and white spirit on the right. Cheap and convenient dispensers.

Mention is made later of the masonry paint used on the cooling tower, and domestic emulsions are quite useful for large-scale and scenic work. Tester pots are a useful source if only small amounts are required.

When I am painting, either by hand or with an airbrush, I am always reaching for either white spirits or IPA either to dilute paints or clean brushes. I have found that keeping some of each in recycled squeezy bottles is very convenient and by having a different style bottle for each, I know exactly what they contain.

AIRBRUSH

Airbrushing is another of those techniques that can seem very daunting to the beginner and it does involve at least a moderate degree of financial outlay too. It is undoubtedly the best way to get a good-quality paint finish using any of the modeller's enamels or acrylics.

EQUIPMENT

Over the years I have acquired three airbrushes, not including my first Humbrol modeller's airbrush, which was a cheap and useful introduction to the art. I have

my faithful Badger 150, which has given many years' service and continues to be frequently used. I also have an Iwata, which gives very fine control. Neither was what you would call inexpensive. Is there a cost-effective alternative for the beginner?

My most recent acquisition, bought as much from curiosity as anything else, is a cheap 'copy' airbrush from eBay for about £16. It looks somewhat like an Iwata design, feels heavy and solid enough, and came with a paint bottle, a paint cup, and three needles and nozzles. With the largest 0.5mm nozzle fitted, it has proved very useful for spraying window frames, brick-effect styrene sheet and for weathering in many of the projects in this book. I've yet to use it to spray a locomotive, but would see no problem in applying a basic colour with it. As an entry point into airbrushing, and as a practice tool, it seems to be remarkable value.

Also required is a source of pressurized air. Aerosol cans are the cheapest starting point and work well enough, though they obviously have a limited capacity and the pressure starts to drop as they discharge.

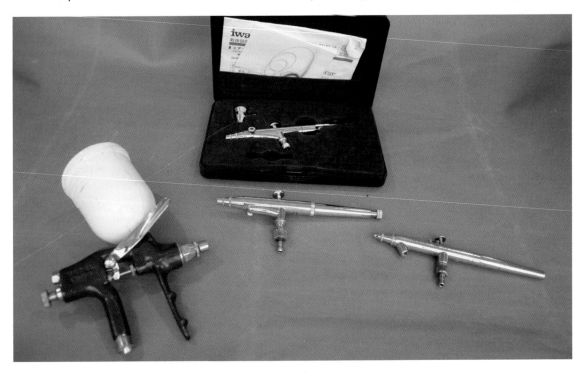

Airbrushes, the cheap 'copy' model sits lower middle. The larger spray gun sees occasional use for weathering large areas.

My compressor with air reservoir. I know that many modeller's use this model.

Start to use a few cans and the cost ramps up. A compressor is really the only option if an airbrush is to be used regularly. The cost of these have dropped in recent years and a small, quiet compressor complete with air reservoir can be obtained for about £70. It is worth paying a little extra for the air reservoir as it evens out fluctuations or pulses in the air pressure.

Finally, some type of spray booth is required as otherwise the overspray will be all over the room. Spray booths in the form of a large cardboard box have been used by me and countless others over the years. They contain most of the overspray, if nothing else. If using just a box it is also wise to use a suitable face mask, one capable of filtering out solvents. As with compressors, inexpensive spray booths with extractor fans and filters have recently become avail-

able. These can trap the paint particles internally, in a filter or, ideally, they can be vented externally. I have used one for a couple of years with satisfactory results and recently improved its performance by providing some ducting through a wall so that any fumes are vented outside. Several of the buildings described in this book were, of course, far too large to fit into any domestic spray booth. Where possible they were painted as smaller components in the booth or, if that was not practical, taken outside for spraying.

So, in summary, it is possible to start off with a sub-£20 airbrush, aerosols to provide air pressure, a cardboard box as a spray booth and a £20 face mask. Later, as funds permit, add a compressor and, if justified, a spray booth.

CHAPTER FIVE

COMMON FEATURES AND DETAILS

In this first constructional chapter we'll look at some industrial structures and features commonly seen at many sites of heavy industry. These are items that are likely to exist in multiples and may be constructed repeatedly by the modeller.

INDUSTRIAL CHIMNEYS

THE PROTOTYPE

Tall factory chimneys once bristled above many of our towns and cities and their associated factories. In the US the phrase 'smokestack industry' is used to describe, usually the older forms, of heavy industry. Two tall chimneys feature in the first photograph in Chapter 1. Chimneys may be just a few tens of feet tall or exceed 1,000ft, i.e. 4m in 4mm scale or 2m in 2mm scale. In 2016, two tall, disused chimneys received some news coverage. The 400ft/122m chimney at Westbury cement works in Wiltshire, as it was being demolished, and an 840ft/250m chimney in Romania because a man was riding a unicycle around its crumbling rim! There are some very tall chimneys out there.

As has been discussed, modelled to scale on the typical area of baseboard available to modellers, such a structure would look completely out of place. Though it might be to the correct scale, in reality such chimneys are seen surrounded by many square miles of real countryside, not a few square feet of baseboard. A prototype around 150ft/46m would be an impressive enough industrial chimney, tall enough to serve most industries and yet be a more manageable 600mm or 300mm in 4mm and 2mm scales, respectively. Setting the height of your tallest chimney gives plenty of scope to model a range of smaller heights for others in order to add variety.

A modern concrete chimney at Ratcliffe-on-Soar power station.

Chimneys can be surprisingly wide at their base. Compare the diameter of this chimney at Port Talbot with the nearby road vehicles. TATA STEEL EUROPE

Several basic forms of chimney exist. Most often circular in cross-section, they can also be square or octagonal, and they may be parallel-sided or have a noticeable taper towards the top. Common construction materials are stone, brick, concrete and steel, the latter being almost universally round in cross-section and parallel-sided. Some Victorian-era chimneys were seen as status symbols by their owners and exhibited various degrees of ornate decoration.

MODEL CHIMNEYS

The modeller is well enough served for chimneys of modest height, certainly in 4mm scale. Kits for brick chimneys are available from some of the Continental kit manufacturers, such as Vollmer, Piko and Faller, who all have brick chimneys, round and square section, in their ranges. The US company Walthers has a nicely moulded brick, round-section chimney in their Cornerstone range. Earlier versions were moulded in two halves but more recently a single-piece model is available, which obviously has no joint line, something that can be difficult to disguise. The author of another book available from The Crowood

A section of moulded plastic chimneys from Walthers and some of the Continental manufacturers. A good variety of designs but none are more than 300mm tall.

Press, David Wright *Making Urban Buildings For Model Railways*, made the masters for a very nice 4mm-scale brick chimney, 260mm tall, which is currently available in resin from Skytrex Model Railways.

However, none of these is more than about 12in or 300mm in height, which is small compared to the type of chimney likely to be serving a prototype textile mill, power station, coke oven battery, large boiler house or steelworks. One ploy to increase the height of a model chimney is to place it on a square base of brick or stone, as with some prototypes. There is a limit to the height of such a base, probably a scale 20ft/6m as a maximum, though a few were taller. Alternatively, if the chimney can be positioned behind the building it serves, so that its lower portion is hidden from view, it can be raised on just a plain column of wood. The column will be hidden by the building itself, with the model chimney soaring above. Do not place a large masonry chimney directly on the roof of a building. A 250ft/8m chimney of brick or stone weighs in excess of one thousand tons and requires very strong foundations. Short, steel chimneys were once a feature of some power stations and they could be mounted on the roof.

MAKING CHIMNEYS FROM SCRATCH

Steel chimneys are relatively easy to produce in model form as they are universally round in cross-section and parallel-sided. Parallel-sided brick and stone chimneys are a little more challenging, whilst the most difficult are tapered brick and stone chimneys. With parallel-sided chimneys, brickpaper or embossed plastic sheet can just be wrapped around and the courses will remain parallel. That will not work with a tapered chimney as the brick courses will not lie horizontal.

MODELLING A STEEL CHIMNEY

Steel chimneys are made up from curved panels of steel sheet riveted or welded together and the panel joints remain visible. Some type of ladder is very often fitted to the side and there may be flanges where prefabricated sections are bolted together. The tops often have reinforcing bands or flanges. Some chimneys may be braced by external wire stays, which are anchored to the ground or to adjacent structure, and the upper portions may feature spiral ribs, which help spread the pressure exerted by strong winds.

A basic steel chimney is a simple modelling task – it's adding the detail that takes the time. Any tubing

Steel chimneys serving the soaking pits at Port Talbot works. TATA STEEL EUROPE

The jig I use for scribing the vertical seams on steel chimneys.

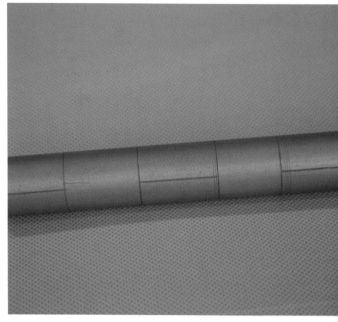

A sample of 20mm conduit pipe scribed to represent individual panels.

can work well: steel or copper, but plastic is the easiest to use.

The six identical chimneys for the open-hearth melting shop project were built in the following manner. Six 480mm lengths were cut from a 20mm plastic conduit using a pull saw and mitre box. A tube cutter was used to scribe horizontal seams every 24mm to represent 6ft panels.

The vertical panel joints were made by marking the end of the tube into six equal segments. A cloth tape-measure can be used to measure around the chimney and to mark out the segments, but it is easy to do by eye, looking down on to the tube end. You may be surprised just how well you can do this.

To scribe the vertical lines I used a jig, which holds the pipe and allows a steel rule to be held firmly on the top. This is a homemade device that makes scribing straight lines along tubing a simple task.

The panels have staggered joints, a brickwork-like effect and the tube was scribed accordingly. The marks placed on the end of the tube determine where the lines are scribed and, by rotating the tube around in the jig, the correct pattern of panel joint lines is achieved. Three vertical lines in each section

of the chimney are staggered over alternate sections. Fine wire-wool was used to clean up the tube, removing any swarf from the scribing, being careful not to overdo it and removing the carefully scribed seam lines.

That will suffice for a perfectly acceptable steel chimney but there are other detailing steps that will further improve it. Conduit tube wall is much too thick to represent steel plate, so thinning out the wall at the top improves the look. This can be done by careful paring with a knife, followed by cleaning up with emery cloth. A hole-enlarging tool, illustrated in Chapter 3, in a cordless drill running at low speed offers a quick and effective alternative. These are available in sets of three and will ream out the end of most plastic tubing likely to be used in modelling. The result is a clean and accurately centred cut.

Flanges to strengthen the top were made from 20 thou styrene sheet. As I didn't have a 20mm hole punch, I punched out an 18mm hole and again used a hole-enlarger running slowly in a cordless drill. The sheet was then placed under a 22mm hole-cutter, aligning the already cut 20mm hole in the centre. This can be done by eye, by just looking down the cutter

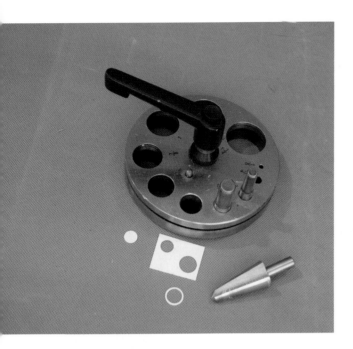

Making thin flanges using the hole punch and hole-enlarging tool.

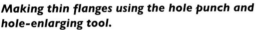

The ladders that I had etched in brass. Each etch contains five ladders and five cages.

hole. Cutting out the larger diameter leaves a narrow flange. This takes a bit of practice and is limited by the hole sizes offered by the punch but enables the production of thin flanges, which would be difficult to produce any other way. One or two ended up off-centre but I soon had the twelve that I needed.

Access ladders take two forms. First, there is a standard ladder fixed to the chimney with simple brackets, which will most likely have a safety cage fitted. To complete the melting shop chimneys I made a first venture into the world of custom brass etching, drawing up the artwork myself and having some caged ladders etched professionally. I was very pleased with the results. I opted for custom-etched ladders rather than using commercial styrene mouldings, as they are much finer and looked better against the slender chimneys.

The second form of ladder sometimes seen on steel chimneys is a run of individual rungs, shaped like large staples, up the side of the chimney. Making the rungs from brass wire is easy enough but fitting them into holes drilled in the chimney requires a good deal more work. Accurate drilling of these holes is essential: a wavy ladder with oddly spaced rungs would not

look good. Should this feature be desired, it might be worth considering making a brass template with the rung-mounting holes, at the desired spacings, drilled into it and then using it to accurately drill the holes in the chimney itself.

A feature of some steel chimneys is a conical base. A flat-topped cone can be cut from styrene sheet and cone calculators to determine the dimensions are available online – just search for 'cone calculator'. Put in the required diameters of the top and base, the height of the cone and the calculator gives the angle and size of the cone as a flat shape. An access door or panel is sometimes fitted into the base so that personnel can enter for inspection, cleaning and maintenance purposes. The chimney, whether or not it has the conical base, will have a heavy flange, which is drilled around the edge, allowing the whole assembly to be bolted to a concrete pad. I cut flanges from 60 thou styrene in exactly the same manner as I had for the top flanges. The heavy nuts and bolts present on this flange can be represented by gluing on small brass nuts or, as I did, using short lengths of styrene rod. These are clearly not so accurate but at a distance they look good enough.

Putting a 'fishmouth' on the end of a length of plastic conduit using a sanding drum in a power drill.

If stay wires are required, simple triangular 'ears' of styrene can be glued to the chimney at the appropriate points and, after installation of the chimney, thin fuse-wire stretched between these and the anchor points will do the job.

The final detail is the incoming flue, linking the base of the chimney with the furnace or boiler that it serves. This may be underground, in which case there is nothing visible other than perhaps an access manhole for maintenance. Flues may be a rectangular section metal box or a cylindrical pipe entering the chimney a few feet above the base. The chimneys being modelled for this project have a cylindrical flue emerging from the melting shop side-wall, which, in the prototype, would link to the waste heat boilers. These boilers utilize the hot waste gasses from the open-hearth furnaces. Short lengths of 20mm conduit were given a 'fish mouth' end using a sanding drum in a bench-mounted electric drill and then superglued on to the chimney. The accompanying photograph should clarify the method.

Steel chimneys can be galvanized or given a metallic paint finish. Mine were simply primed with a car paint aerosol, followed by spraying with appropriate aluminium colour aerosol to finish. The tops often have a black finishing band, which is easily applied with masking tape and a black spray. Other chimneys are painted in a matt black finish, though this is better represented as a dark grey.

Even if modelling a new chimney, the seam lines need highlighting with a basic weathering technique. Each chimney was given a wash of a very dilute solution of gunmetal enamel, allowing it to run into the scribed seams and the excess was then wiped off with a thinners-dampened kitchen towel. Wiping downwards follows the pattern of rain streaking. Downward steaks of grime and rust were applied at the horizontal seams and by any brackets and fittings. Black chimneys will benefit from a very light spray of rust, which will bring the finish to life. The chimney top will need some evidence of soot, so a spray of a soft dark grey around the top and interior will finish it off nicely. As the project chimneys are to serve an open-hearth melting shop, and the smoke they emit contains a large amount of iron oxide, a dark rusty orange needs to be applied too.

The chimneys sit on concrete pads made from 5mm foamboard. At present these are not firmly

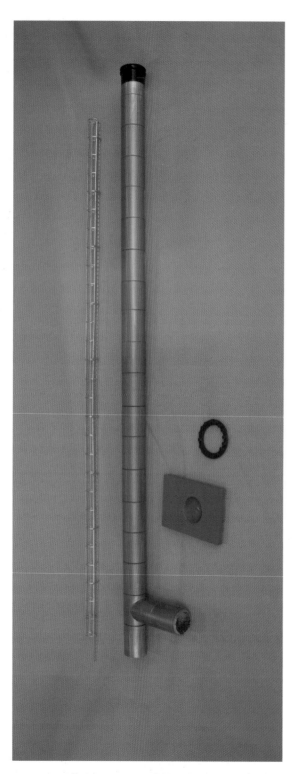

fixed; the tall chimneys are vulnerable and until the melting shop is finally installed, they will be removed for storage.

MODELLING CONCRETE AND BRICK CHIMNEYS

Small chimneys are well enough catered for by available kits and the modeller in 2mm scale could well utilize 4mm-scale models. However, I was in need of something a good deal larger.

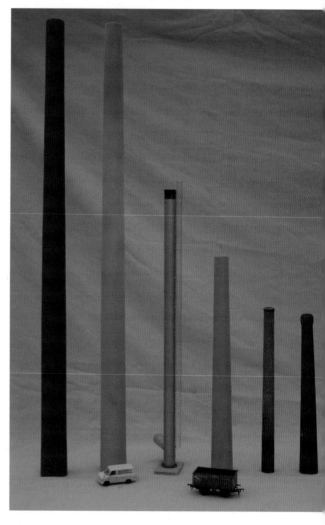

The components for the steel chimneys seen assembled in Chapter 14.

A comparison between the heights of some model chimneys. From right to left: Walthers, Vollmer, a cut down turning, a fabricated steel chimney and two 750mm chimneys made from custom wood turnings.

The basis for this build is a turned wooden former. Some modeller's may have the facilities to turn up something suitable in their own workshops, or may have friends who can. If not, there may be a local wood-turner or wood-turning club. These days an internet search under 'wood turner' and a locality will find them. Another option is to buy a suitable ready turned table leg; they can be found on eBay, but there are limits to the sizes available. I have some turned table legs for later projects but for this project I had a wood-turning company turn up half a dozen tapered spindles. These are 750 mm long, 35mm diameter at the top and 45mm at the base. When I received them I drilled out their tops to replicate the hollow centres and thin walls of a real chimney.

Two of these, at full height, will be used as coke-oven chimneys and, at 750mm tall, they represent prototypes of around 190ft/58m, which is smaller than a typical 250ft/76m chimney but imposing enough. By cutting them short, either at the top or the bottom or both, I have some flexibility in making chimneys with different heights and proportions.

The spindles were given a light sanding before being sprayed with primer. The simplest finish is concrete, achieved with a thin coat of the masonry paint mix followed by spraying with suede-effect paint.

Brick presents more of a challenge. I have produced a trial model by wrapping narrow, 25mm strips of Scalescenes' brickpaper around the chimney. The taper is not so pronounced and it is just possible to hide the sloping brickwork courses. However, experiments continue to perfect a method. One is to try printing brickwork on decal paper and then using a setting solution to give some stretch to the paper. My preferred method would be to print out brickpaper in a conical pattern designed to exactly match the profile of the wooden former.

PIPEWORK, VALVES AND FITTINGS

A characteristic feature of heavy industry is the festooning of plant and buildings with pipework of various diameters and its associated valves and fittings, the

Pipework on gantries at Lancashire Steels' Irlam works. TATA STEEL EUROPE

whole offering a bewildering tangle. If it's not attached to a building, pipework seems to run freely, hither and thither, across the whole works' site.

Such pipework carries a whole range of gasses and fluids. The most common are water, both hot and cold, water under pressure for hydraulic service, steam, gas for fuel and compressed air. Others are oxygen, carbon dioxide and any number of other chemicals and gasses used in various industrial processes. The industry you model will determine just what pipework will be required and what it would carry. Some works colour-code pipework, either by painting the whole pipe or colour banding it at regular intervals, to aid staff with identifying what the pipe carries but there is no universally accepted convention for these colours.

IS IT PIPE OR IS IT TUBE?

There is no definitive difference between pipe and tube. It might be thought that the diameter or the wall thickness or some technical specification differentiates one from the other, but this is not the case. The terms pipe and tube are interchangeable and it is the convention preferred by the end-user that applies. What one user calls pipe, another may call tube. There are some generalizations; larger sections tend to be referred to as pipe, as do cast-iron hollow sections.

Once the UKs largest maker of 'hollow steel sections', Stewarts & Lloyds referred to themselves as tube makers, yet their catalogues, aimed at various trades, described their products in the language of that consumer, e.g. tube for boilermakers, pipe for gas engineers. A British Steel Corporation, Tubes Division, handbook from 1971 states in the glossary, 'Pipe; see Tube' and under Tube 'A parallel-sided hollow cylinder with open ends. The terms tube and pipe are synonymous'. G. R. Bashforth, writing an introduction to the rolling of steel tube in a textbook entitled *The Manufacture of Iron and Steel, Vol. 4* (Chapman & Hall, 1962), stated 'it is customary to refer to certain steel hollows as tubes and to others as pipes generally according to the purpose for which they are to be used... during the process of their manufacture all these components are described as tubes, irrespective of their ultimate usage'.

SOURCES OF MODELLING TUBE

Tube suitable for modelling is available in copper, brass and a variety of plastics; each has benefits and drawbacks. For straight runs, devoid of bends, copper pipe is useful. It's available in long lengths and is delivered nice and straight, is easy to scribe, to cut and to solder. On the other hand there are only three commonly available diameters: 10, 15 and 22mm. The matching fittings and bends, etc., soldered or compression, look nothing like prototype pipework bends, and copper pipe is not cheap. It probably is only worthwhile using if a supply of redundant plumbing is forthcoming. Brass tube has similar drawbacks; it is generally available only in shorter lengths, though a wider range of diameters is available. It does have a nice thin wall, which can be useful for applications where there will be an open end. I am not aware of any fittings being available for this thin-walled brass tubing.

Plastic tubing is, generally speaking, a much more useable option. The first consideration is the type of plastic the pipe is made from. That supplied for modellers, generally less than 25mm diameter, is

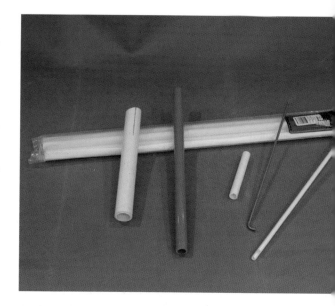

A variety of plastic tube suitable for modelling purposes. Electrical conduit, tube from Plastruct and Evergreen, solid 'pipe' from Knightwing and salvaged sprue from a kit.

made from styrene. This type of styrene tube is available from Plastruct and Evergreen and unbranded from China via the internet. Plastruct in particular sell matching bends, elbows, Ts, etc., which look like the prototype. Plastic is, of course, easy to cut, sand and shape, joins very strongly with readily available solvents and takes paint well. There are also kits for pipe and fittings for smaller pipes available from Knightwing in the UK and Walthers in the US. In fact, they are exactly the same mouldings. These kits are very useful, if only for the fittings they contain, which can be used in conjunction with the plain tube from the likes of Evergreen.

Another source is the sprues from injection-moulded plastic kits. Not all are suitable but some are fully round in section and often include nicely radiused corners and Tees. They require a bit of cleaning up but are free and would otherwise be discarded.

Other plastic pipe, made for plumbing, drainage and electrical conduit purposes, provides some useful larger sizes, though it is sometimes made from plastics that are not the easiest to glue, and the long lengths it is sold in may have a slight curve to them. Leaving them to lie flat or, better still, hanging them vertically, will straighten them out. This type of pipe is cheap to buy and ideal for long, straight runs but the fittings sold for it have no application in modelling. If you use these fittings, the result will look like what it is: domestic plumbing rather than industrial pipework. These fittings are designed to slide over the pipe and be fixed with solvent adhesive. Prototype industrial pipe fittings are of the same diameter as the pipe and they are attached by welding or by bolted flanges.

WORKING WITH PLASTIC PIPEWORK

Straight Pipe

Simply cut to length with a mitre saw, or any fine-toothed saw, in a mitre box and then clean the ends with fine abrasive paper. The tube cutters are used to represent welded joints in lengths of pipework. As noted in Chapter 3, these are not the best tools to cut plastic tube with as the tube tends to flatten under the pressure. Longitudinal joints or seams can, with care, be scribed on plastic tube using a steel straight edge and a scalpel or scriber. However, if a large amount of tube is to be scribed, a homemade jig will speed up the process. I have a couple of such jigs. One I use for scribing 20 and 25mm conduit tube and which is illustrated on page 51, where it is being used to prepare a steel chimney. The larger jig will accept any tube between 65 to 100mm outside diameter and this is used to prepare tanks and silos such as those featured in Chapter 7.

Bends

Welded fittings are of the same diameter as the pipe itself. The easiest, though most costly, way to model bends and other fittings is to use those available in piping kits or those from Plastruct.

To make a simple right-angle bend from solid or hollow round-section, use a mitre block to cut the two pipe ends to 45 degrees and join them with solvent. When fully dry, put a fillet of plastic filler into the right angle of the joint and allow to dry. Finally, sand a smooth curve into the angle, adding filler as required. A suitable bit of kit sprue might do the job for you.

Various bends, 'T' and valves from Plastruct.

Gusseted Bends

On prototype larger diameter pipework, prefabricated bends are often not available and bends are made by cutting angled segments and welding a number of these together to form the desired angle of bend. Fortunately, on the prototype, the costs of

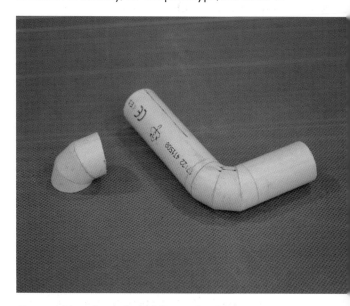

Gusseted bends made in 20mm plumbing tube. Some examples of finished gusseted bends can be seen in some of the finished models.

doing this are related to the number of segments used, so they tend to use as few as possible. To make a 90-degree segmented bend, three, more often four and sometimes six segments are used, which makes the modeller's job that bit easier. For modelling projects, gusseted bends are made just like the prototype. V-shaped sections of pipe are cut using a mitre box setting the angle to suit the number of segments required. Cutting these small lengths with angled ends does take some care. The Proxxon modeller's mitre saw considerably speeds up the process, especially as the tube, once clamped in the vice, is held on the same line and can be rotated to cut the opposing angles. It is a high-quality tool, but it is an expensive piece of equipment costing considerably more than many workshop-sized mitre saws. This really is an example of a tool that only an anticipated extensive use can justify.

PROTOTYPE VALVES

There are several types of industrial valves in use. The simplest just has a circular disc housed within the valve body that can be turned across the flow to stop it. When the valve is open, the disc sits within the flow, edge on. They have an obvious bulk but little other external detail other than the operating wheel.

A visibly larger valve is the gate valve. This has a screw-operated sliding diaphragm that can be completely withdrawn from the pipe to open it or it can be screwed in to close off the flow.

A much larger valve is the spectacle or goggle valve. This resembles a pair of spectacles having two circular frames fixed together. One frame is the valve body, which sits in line with the pipeline, whilst the other projects off it. A circular diaphragm hinged between the frames can be moved quickly from one frame to the other, opening or closing the valve.

MAKING VALVES

A simple way of representing a valve is to slide a larger diameter length of tube over the pipe-line tube, adding a flange at either end with a body and handwheel from a kit. Plastic putty can be used to bulk out a rounded valve body.

A simple valve made up from styrene punchings and two sizes of tube. Handwheels can be sourced from the Knightwing piping kits and from etched frets.

A gate valve also made up from styrene sheet, strip and tube.

Gate valves can be fabricated from styrene sheet and section. The valve body is made from two rectangles of 40 thou styrene stuck together. They have holes punched at one end to fit over the pipe and this end is sanded into a semi-circle. The top end has its shoulders rounded off. Four narrow strips of styrene fitted around the body form a flange where the top and bottom halves of the valve would be bolted together. The gland and valve spindle fitted to the top are from styrene tube and rod with a handwheel from a brass etch or plastic kit. For a motorized valve, short lengths of round and square tube form a motor and gearbox assembly.

A spectacle valve, generally found on larger diameter pipework, is a more complex assembly, though they are, fortunately, not so common. I wouldn't scratchbuild one of these as Alkem Models in the US make a suitable laser-cut kit.

COMMERCIALLY AVAILABLE VALVES

The Knightwing and Walthers kits provide some perfectly acceptable small valves. Plastruct have a range of valves in their catalogue. Some are rather representational in that they clip on and do not provide a complete flange. However, they are a good starting point for further detailing. Peachcreek Models in the US supply a range of items for the industrial modeller. Amongst these is their own range of sliding-gate valve kits, which are designed to match Plastruct pipework. They also supply the Alkem range of valve kits; lovely laser-cut kits for spectacle valves

SADDLES, PIPE RACKS AND BRIDGES

Though circular sections are very strong they still need support over long runs. Pipework at ground level will be supported on saddles, and groups of pipes on saddles grouped into pipe racks. A saddle is simply a support shaped to cup around and support the pipe, and these in turn are mounted on a frame or rack, providing structural support. Commonly, pipework hangs off the side of buildings, again supported on saddles, with the saddles resting on steelwork cantilevered off the building's support structure. This type of arrangement is very common in industrial situations.

Pipe bridges are used to carry pipes across open ground but raised up to allow road and rail traffic to pass beneath. Very long runs of such raised pipework are not uncommon. Laid on the ground they would present an impenetrable barrier to traffic within the works. The nature of the bridge depends, naturally, on the weight carried and can range from slender lattice towers to massive structural uprights with truss or plate girder horizontals.

Saddles are modelled from styrene sheet. Whenever I punch out a disc, I keep the punched sheet. By cutting a square around it and then cutting it diagonally into four I have saddles to fit a matching

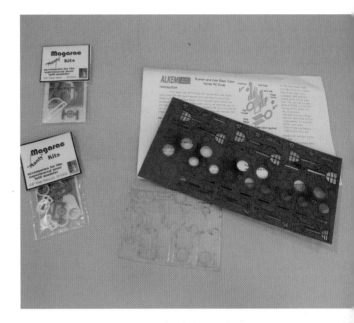

Commercially available valves from Peachcreek models and Alkem Models in the US.

The components for a simple pipe-support saddle.

Pipework supported on brackets cantilevered off the side of a building. The brackets are simple assemblies from lengths of styrene sections and Plastruct truss. A large gusseted bend is also visible.

diameter of tube. Sometimes I make them for the job in hand, in which case the disc is kept for later use. The saddles can be used like that or detailed with styrene strip flanges and strengthening ribs.

Pipe racks are frameworks made up from styrene sections as needed, as are cantilevered supports for use on buildings.

Bridge supports can be made up from styrene section into any shape, size and mass as required. Various kits can provide suitable parts. Dapols, ex-Airfix, signal gantry kit provides two uprights and footbridge kits from several manufacturers to provide heavy duty support structures. Horizontal support framework, if required, can be made up from Evergreen sections or cannibalized from commercial bridge kits. For 4mm scale, N gauge bridge parts are suitable and for 7mm scale both 4 and 2mm kit parts are suitable.

FENCING

All industrial plants will be fenced off from their neighbours, from the public and from any adjacent railways. There may also be certain parts of the plant within the overall boundary that are individu-

ally fenced off. This limits access, perhaps because the plant within is sensitive or dangerous, or it may contain materials of great value.

The two most common types of industrial fencing are concrete posts with chain-link mesh or concrete posts with concrete-panel infill, both usually with three strands of barbed wire across the top. The mesh, or concrete panelling, is often 6ft/2m high but may be anything up to 12ft/4m high and even higher at very high-security establishments. Some years ago I had a spell of erecting this sort of fencing around a number of industrial facilities in the north-west. Chain-link fencing features heavy section corners and straining posts, both of which have concrete bracing struts aligned to the fence line. These posts take the strain of the horizontal wires stretched taut between them. The lighter intermediate posts just give vertical support to the wires and mesh. Two points are worth making. Neither the barbed wire nor the horizontal straining wires run through the holes in the posts but they lie flush on the outer faces. They are held fast there by a U-shaped length of wire, which does pass through the holes which is then bent forwards and bound tightly around the horizontal wires. Second, if, as is usually the case, the posts have

An example of the ubiquitous chain-link fencing that separates us from many sites of heavy industry.

Chain-link fencing from Ratio on my Staplegrove module. Using a brass post every so often enables a reasonable amount of strain to be put on the horizontal wires, though they will sag after a while.

angled tops, they must not overhang the property boundary. This means, if the property owner wants the fence along their boundary, the overhang must be inwards. If the overhang is to be on the outside, for maximum security, the fence must be stepped back from the boundary. The former is by far the more usual arrangement. Ratio supply a chain-link fencing kit that provides a quick and easy solution and was used on the Staplegrove module.

POST AND PANEL FENCING

This also uses concrete posts cast in an H-section. Once the posts are in place, long concrete panels are dropped in between the posts, the groove in the H-section holding them firm. They are usually finished with three strands of barbed wire. This is very easily made from styrene sheet, with strip and square section styrene for the posts.

I use 60 x 60 thou square rod for the heavier end and corner posts. The panelling is made from appropriate lengths of 40 thou styrene sheet cut 24mm high and scribed longitudinally at 4mm spacing to

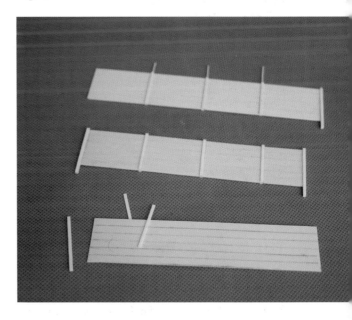

Components for making up a length of concrete post and panel fencing. The finished result can be seen at the rear of the laboratory in Chapter 9.

Modern steel paling fencing, which seems to be the current barrier of choice.

represent 6in concrete panels. Intermediate posts are narrow strips of styrene; one aligned each side at 32mm intervals. A little cube of styrene placed between these strips, at the top, gives the look of H-section posts. The rear yard of the laboratory featured in Chapter 9 features some finished post and panel fencing.

STEEL PALING FENCING

This type of fencing has become the modern replacement for chain-link fencing. It consists of shaped steel uprights, with spikes formed at the top, bolted to steel horizontals and with steel posts. It can either be painted or galvanized. Knightwing Security Fencing, kit PM121, provides an excellent model of this in 4mm scale and I cannot think of a simple way of scratchbuilding it better.

CONVEYOR BELTS

THE PROTOTYPE

Many large industrial sites utilize conveyor belts to move bulk materials. They have limitations but where large volumes of materials need to be moved from and to fixed points, and over long periods of time, conveyors offer a very efficient method of transport. Materials typically handled by conveyors are coal and coke, minerals, stone and ores, grain and woodchip, all materials likely to be used in very large quantities. Building conveyors over very long distances that are measured in miles, is unusual, though not unknown; rail would generally be the preferred choice for longer distances. Conveyors also tend to be dedicated to the movement of a single material.

As well as providing lateral transport, conveyors are widely used to elevate materials into storage bunkers or silos. Modern blast furnaces are also charged by conveyor systems, the currently idle furnace at Redcar being an example. Most conveyor systems employ flat, flexible belts running over rollers, with the outer rollers being canted upwards, to form a shallow trough shape. The maximum gradient at which a conveyor will operate is determined by the nature of the materials being moved. It does not take much imagination to realize that smooth, round objects would just roll back on the belt at even a shallow angle, whereas coarse, irregular lumps would more likely 'lock' together and so can be carried at steeper angles. Tables of maximum conveyor angles for a variety of bulk materials are available and the system would be built to suit. Belts can be provided with ridges to increase the maximum angle of inclination. Clearly conveyor belts cannot move materials around corners and to overcome this

A boom stacker at Port Talbot Steelworks. It takes ore off the belt feeding in from the left, and distributes it onto storage piles on either side. TATA STEEL EUROPE

limitation, conveyor belt systems incorporate transfer stations where the first belt delivers the material on to the start of a second belt situated below it. This second belt can be built running off in any direction. Belts often run over and serve a number of separated storage bunkers. In such situations a 'tripper' will be incorporated. This is a device that moves along the belt and diverts the materials off it and into the appropriate bunker. These are often under cover, as with the coal-blending bunker project, and so need not be modelled.

Where conveyors serve storage or stacking grounds it is often useful for the belt to be moveable and to have a means of distributing the material over a wide area. A boom stacker is one such device and one is illustrated here.

MODELLING CONVEYOR BELTS

Walthers make two models of conveyor belts and they are a quick and easy method of making the open type – those without side cladding.

For those belts with corrugated cladding, usually asbestos sheeting, on their sides I make up an inner beam of foamboard strips, glued together. I then clad this in Wills asbestos cladding, inserting etched window-frames at regular intervals.

Transfer stations are made up in the same manner. Lattice steel support towers for both the belts and transfer stations can be made up from styrene section or cannibalized from kit components. Footbridge and signal gantry kits often contain something suitable.

STAIRWAYS, WALKWAYS AND LADDERS

As with pipework, much of heavy industry appears to be draped with walkways, ladders and stairways allowing access to every nook and cranny. Clearly, it always serves a purpose; linking levels, linking adjacent structures or providing access to elevated bits of plant and equipment.

In reality walkways and step treads are often made up from steel mesh, which allows water to drain and provides a good grip. I just make walkways from strips of 40 thou styrene, supported along the edge with vertical strips of styrene forming a shallow channel. Depending on the structure, I use this channel either way up and form handrails from 40 x 40 thou for the uprights and with 30 x 20 thou for the handrails. Plastruct make pre-formed handrails but the fixed positioning of the uprights will rarely suit the needs of a particular model such that the spacing can look odd.

A short sample of covered conveyor made from foamboard and Wills sheets. The top is Slater's corrugated, which readily takes a curve, though the 7mm corrugated sheet would be a better match for the Wills sheet. Make them as long as required.

An example of a walkway and stairway on the Staplegrove module.

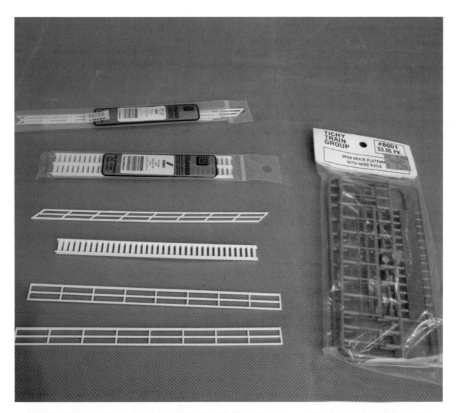

Commercially available stairways and walkways. The Tichy Trains' walkways feature see-through grating – nice but not that obvious once installed.

A landing between two lengths of stairway on the gas-holder.

Plastic caged ladders from Walthers and Plastruct.

Conversely, I wouldn't use anything other than Plastruct's open stairways, which are well moulded and do the job very well. For the same reason as outlined above, I don't use their matching handrails preferring to build my own.

Landings provide relief on long stairways, allow the stairs to turn corners or provide access to the structure being served. These are made in the same way as walkways being shaped to suit their position.

Caged ladders, those with a safety structure around them, are a very common feature on industrial structures. Models are available from Plastruct and Walthers. I've used both to good effect and they are simple to assemble and to fit to a model. Large amounts can prove a little costly and they might be considered a little 'heavy' in aspect. Having tried Gold Medal etched caged ladders on the water tower project in this book I was pleased with the much finer appearance. They are not that readily available in the UK and are relatively expensive. I decided to have some ladders and cages etched and drew up my own artwork using desktop publishing software.

This had a grid drawing function and it was very easy to draw up grids of simple horizontal and vertical lines and to manipulate their proportions to produce good ladder and cage shapes. The results exceeded my expectations and can be seen on the melting shop chimneys in Chapter 14.

Fitting ladders, walkways and stairways can be quite a time-consuming task. A great deal of cutting and fitting, using templates and trial and error, are required. Some support framework or structural members will also be required, which adds to the size of the task but also adds a satisfying amount of clutter and complexity to the finished model.

CONCLUSION

Whatever model you choose to build, incorporate some chimneys, plenty of pipework and walkways, a conveyor or two, and it will very strongly suggest heavy industry. None of them are industry-specific but all are structures very strongly associated with our mental image of heavy industry.

CHAPTER SIX

GAS-HOLDER OR GASOMETER

THE PROTOTYPE

Gas-holder or gasometer? The correct term, the one used in related technical documentation, is gas-holder, which describes exactly what these structures do. However, the term gasometer, which rather more suggests a metering device of some form, is very widely used and has been for very many years. It may well originate from one of the Victorian pioneers of the gas industry, William Murdoch, who named his gas-storage vessels after a small chamber used in laboratories and known by the French name *gazometre*.

The function of a gas-holder is to store gas and to act as a buffer between production and demand. Until the end of the twentieth century, gas-holders were a common sight across our towns and cities, and even in some larger villages. Their number has drastically reduced over recent years. They are less relevant in an age where gas is no longer manufactured but is taken direct from underground reserves. The vast gas grid, the network of underground pipes delivering gas across the country, has sufficient volume in itself to act as a reservoir.

Most of these structures stood at gasworks where gas was generated from coal for supply to commercial and domestic customers. They could also be found at some petrochemical complexes. The last remaining functioning gas-holders stand at large steelworks where they hold gas derived from coke ovens and blast furnaces; both used as fuel within the works themselves.

TYPES OF GAS-HOLDER

Over the years a number of different designs have been used and many were familiar landmarks across the country. So much so that a number have been given listed status.

LOW-PRESSURE VESSELS

There are two types of low-pressure gas-holders and, because they hold the gas at low pressure, they are generally very large and very obvious. These are the gas-holders with which most people will be familiar.

Water-Seal Gas-Holders

These are the older Victorian designs that incorporate telescoping sections, which were originally made from wrought iron and, once it became cheaply available, steel. They are the archetypal gas-holder: enormous fat tanks, often with a surrounding steel lattice framework, slowly rising and then falling like the lungs of the city. Water-filled troughs between each section allow them to slide in relation to each other whilst retaining a gas-tight seal. The holders themselves sit in a water-filled pond, some of which

The surviving framework of a water seal gas-holder at Aston, Birmingham.

are very deep, allowing the whole of the telescoping holder to sink into the ground. Some have a fixed lower section that remains visible even if the holder is empty. As gas is pumped in, the sections rise to accommodate it and the weight of these sections provides a pressure to the gas within.

On the original designs, the gas-holding vessel is surrounded by a lattice work comprising substantial vertical members, connected by lateral supporting members and cross-bracing. The sections rise vertically, being guided by wheels running up the inside of vertical structural members. This fixed framework around the gas-holder is visible whether or not the gas-holder is full, often standing stark and bare against the skyline. A later design dispensed with the external framework and the individual sections rise and fall on integral spiral guides instead. When these holders are empty, and the sections are collapsed into each other, they are barely visible.

Waterless Gas-Holders

The other common type was the 'waterless gas-holder', a design that has been around since the 1920s. The distinctive feature of these is that their external appearance and size does not change whether they are full or empty. Rather than having telescoping sections, they have an internal piston that rises on internal guides within the fixed outer shell as the gas is pumped in. They have a characteristic tall aspect and seem, almost universally, to be painted a pale blue colour. There are at least three designs. The most common in the UK were those of the German MAN design. These are polygonal in cross-section having flat facets on their sides, anything between eight and sixteen, possibly more, with prominent horizontal ribs around them. A system of flexible seals lubricated with oil and tar provides a gas-tight seal between the piston and the holder walls. The MAN type could be seen at urban gasworks and steelworks across the country; the one that stood until recently at Battersea gasworks being one of the more famous examples.

Less commonly seen is another German design, the Klonne type, which has the horizontal ribbing but is round in cross-section and which uses grease to

A MAN-type waterless gas-holder, which once stood on the Wirral.

lubricate the gas seal. Some of this type saw use at a number of UK steelworks, e.g. Port Talbot.

A more modern development, dating from 1952, is the dry-seal Wiggins' type, which uses a rubber membrane screen to provide a flexible gas-tight seal. These are circular in cross-section and also feature horizontal ribbing.

Used at large urban gasworks, waterless gas-holders are also the type most commonly seen at steelworks. They are used to hold both coke-oven and blast-furnace gas, and have capacities measured in millions of cubic feet. MAN and Klonne holders have been built with capacities of over half a million cubic metres. They were built in many sizes, a few at less than 30m tall but most at around 60 or 70m.

HIGH-PRESSURE VESSELS

The advantage of storing gas at high pressure is that the storage vessels can be a lot smaller for the same storage volume. Again, there are two types.

Spherical Gas-Holders

The earlier type of high-pressure holder made use of the inherent strength of a sphere. In the UK this design is almost entirely confined to petrochemical sites. Holders of this type are spherical steel globes supported on eight or so vertical legs with a spiral access stairway winding up their flanks.

Bullet Gas-Holders

A once common type in the UK is the 'bullet' gas-holder: long, horizontal tanks with domed ends. Incredibly strongly built, they hold very large volumes of gas at very high pressure and many were brought into use during the 1960s and 1970s. Despite their small and unobtrusive nature, doubts began to grow about the wisdom of storing gas at very high pressures, especially in urban environments. These doubts

Bullet-type high pressure gas-holders at Partington, west of Manchester.

strengthened following the detonating of bombs by the IRA at a gas-storage facility in Warrington in 1993. Fortunately there were no injuries and the bullet tanks at the site were undamaged. Councils began to insist that, if built at all, bullet-type tanks should be sited well away from urban areas. However, in recent years, such concerns have become somewhat irrelevant as the need to store gas has diminished.

As mentioned earlier, gas-holders of all types are rapidly disappearing from our landscapes and soon the only working examples will be those at steelworks and petrochemical plants. A few have gained protected status, such as the one overlooking the Oval cricket ground, and will remain as monuments to once familiar sights and industrial processes.

MODELLING GAS-HOLDERS

AVAILABLE MODELS

Models for spherical gas-holders have been available in both N and H0 scales from European manufacturers for some while. At one time Model Power sold a small, ready-made, externally framed gas-holder. Walthers offer a framed, water-seal gas-holder in their Cornerstone range and Hornby also have a small version in their Skaledale range. The latter would really only suit a large village gasworks. Most recently, and still available, Bachmann offer a MAN-style gas-holder in their Scenecraft range.

All of these suffer the inevitable compromise that the manufacturer has to make between a usable model and the sheer size of the prototype. In fact, the Walthers kit aside, they are really too small to be anything other than a pastiche of the real thing.

BUILDING A WATERLESS GAS-HOLDER

The project model is intended to represent a MAN-type gas-holder built in half-relief. Proportions estimated from a large number of photographs suggested that, typically, the diameter of such structures is about 60 per cent of their height. This proportion is important in planning the model so that the final result captures the look of the prototype. Using this proportion and considering the space available, a model 650mm tall and 400mm in diameter was decided on, having a sixteen-sided polygonal cross-section. The model was planned to be a little over half-relief with ten of the sixteen sides modelled, the rear being flat to stand against the backscene. A simple outline was drawn on a large piece of graph paper to check the proportions and to get a feel for the size and bulk of the final model.

THE MAIN BODY

Construction commenced by drawing a circle of radius 400mm on to a piece of 4mm MDF board and, using a compass and pencil, dividing it into sixteen equal segments. The flat facets were drawn across

the ends of these segments and a line drawn across the whole to mark off ten of them.

This shape was then cut out using a heavy craft knife. It forms both the base and acts as a template for the horizontal formers. A rectangle of 4mm MDF, as wide as the rear of the template and as high as the planned gas-holder body, was also cut out.

The polygonal template was then used to cut out five horizontal formers from 10mm foamboard, one being subsequently glued to this MDF former.

The plan was to build a substructure for the gas-holder consisting of these five horizontal formers separated by vertical risers, the risers being simple foamboard boxes. Four strips of 10mm foamboard, 140mm deep, were cut out; these strips were cut into panels and formed into four-sided boxes.

The basic MDF former marked ready for cutting the flat sides.

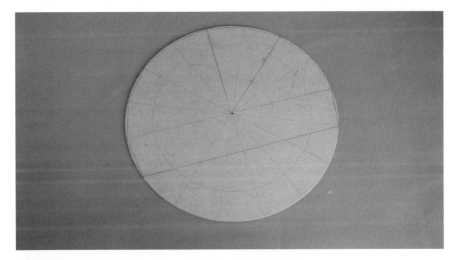

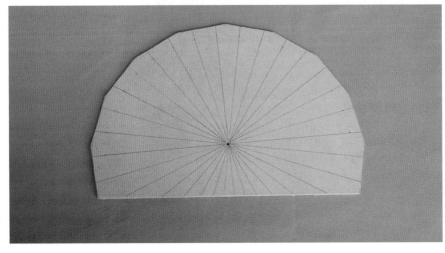

The former with the sides cut and the rear removed.

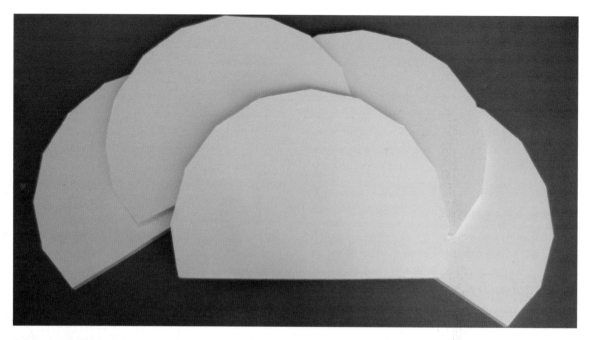

The foamboard formers cut using the MDF former as a template.

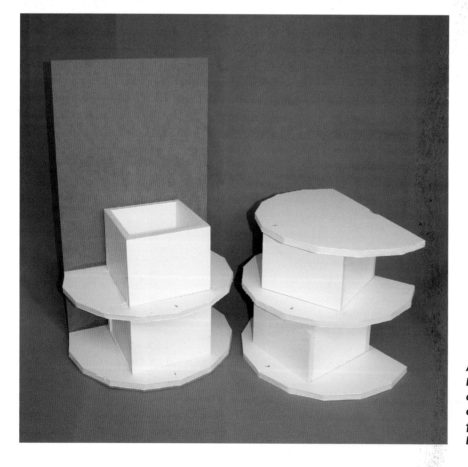

Assembly of the basic tower with an MDF backboard and the foamboard formers spaced out by foamboard risers.

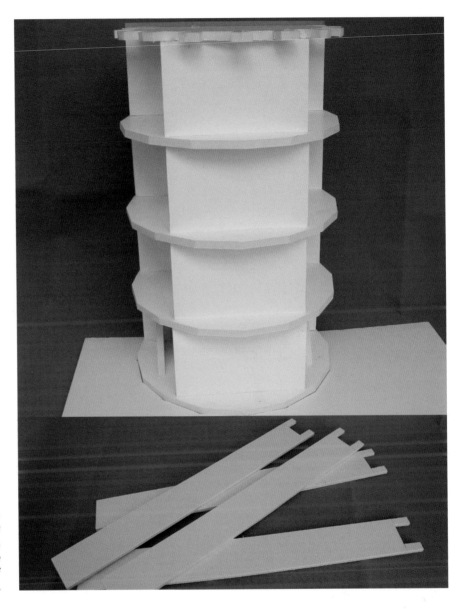

Completed basic tower with cut-outs in the top former to clear the windows.

Foamboard strips, also with cut outs for the windows, which formed the flat sides of the gas-holder.

The basic support tower could now be assembled with the MDF back glued at a right angle to the base. A square riser section was glued to the base and a horizontal former glued on the top and to the backboard. In order to keep everything square, this assembly was carefully checked and allowed to dry, again overnight. With a firm and square foundation, the rest of the support tower could then be assembled.

The side-panel supports were cut from 5mm foamboard. A little trial and error was undertaken to ensure the panels were of the same width and, when aligned, that they accurately covered the face of the support structure. A rectangle was cut out of the top edge to accommodate the windows. Matching sections were cut out of the top former for the same reason. This is one of the benefits of using foamboard since it cuts so readily that modifications can easily be made as construction progresses.

The panels were laid flat on the work bench, lined up and then joined on their rear faces with strips of masking tape.

With the support tower laid on its back, the side panels can be draped over it, rather like a length of caterpillar track, and glued on with PVA. This method keeps the side panels nicely in line whilst allowing time for adjustment. Accurate alignment now helps considerably with the later stages.

As the foamboard panels are draped around the formers, gaps naturally open up between each adjacent pair and they will form location points for the vertical support members. These were made from Evergreen strip, inserted into these gaps and held with UHU.

The foamboard strips laid flat and held as a single piece using masking tape.

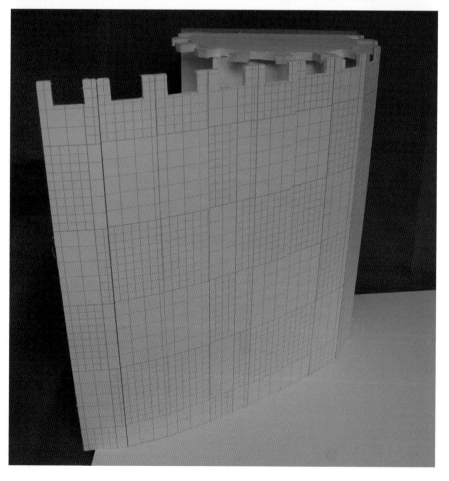

Trial fitting of the sides to the inner tower. Final fitting with PVA was done with the tower lying on its back.

Vertical ribs of Evergreen strip being fitted into the gaps, which open up when the side panels are draped around the inner tower.

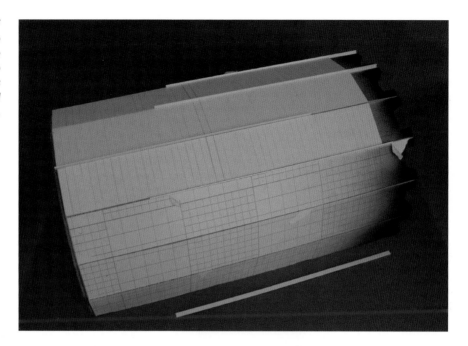

Viewing the prototype, it might be thought that they are built with flat-sheet sides between vertical members and strengthened by horizontal ribs. In fact they are made from a special steel section cut to length to fit between the vertical members with the sections welded one above the other until the required height is reached.

Copying this method of individual panels would not be a practical way of building a model. It would be difficult to keep the sides flat and would be very time-consuming. The model was constructed using flat styrene panels with the horizontal ribs represented by styrene strip.

The outer faces of the holder were clad in 40 thou styrene cut from A3 sheets to minimize the number of joints required. Only a single joint was required and each top section had an aperture 20 x 20mm cut into it for the windows.

Prior to cutting out the individual panels, the whole sheet was marked across with horizontal pencil lines 10mm apart to act as guidelines for fixing the horizontal ribbing. The strips were then cut out and carefully laid on the gas-holder sides, between the vertical ribs. The foamboard used for the sides had an adhesive face, and with the backing paper pulled away, the styrene panels were held in place.

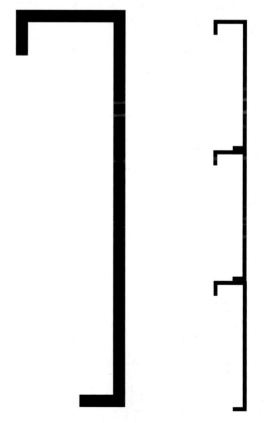

The steel profile used in the construction of MAN-type gas-holders.

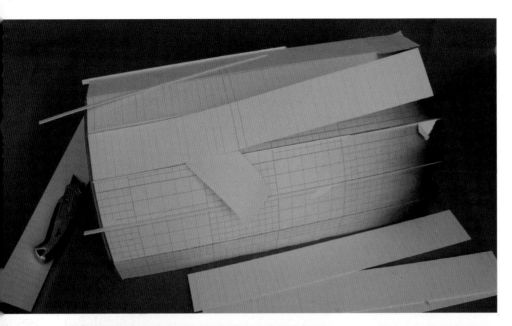

Plastic facing panels were stuck to the foamboard sides. This was a rare occasion when I used adhesive backed foamboard. The strips lying in the foreground show the horizontal pencil lines to help apply the horizontal ribbing.

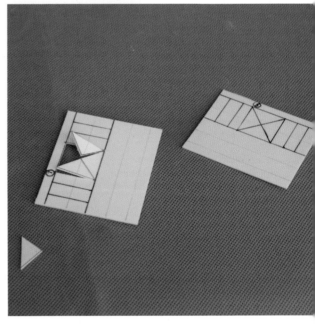

ABOVE: *The top plastic panel which contains the window aperture.*

LEFT: *Horizontal rib application under way. The triangular object is the spacer made from two pieces of 5mm MDF.*

Plain foamboard and UHU glue would have achieved the same end. The edges of the styrene panels were then fixed to the vertical ribs by running solvent down the joint.

With the vertical supports fitted and the external cladding in place, the next task was to cut and fit the individual horizontal ribs. The model required almost 500, which were cut from styrene strip, with the ends appropriately angled, using the NWSL Chopper featured in Chapter 3. Previous efforts to keep everything square, aligned and symmetrical now pay dividends as, ideally, all of the ribs should be identical and so should be more easily cut in bulk. Most likely, a little variation will have crept in during assembly and some checking and fitting will be required as the ribs are fixed with solvent. They were spaced at 10mm intervals, which gave a good appearance; a simple jig from MDF ensured accuracy. This is a slow and tedious process best done over several sessions. It is critical to keep the ribs level and in line to capture the look of the prototype. Eventually, and with a sense of relief and satisfaction, the final rib will be positioned. Styrene strip was used for the strengthening ribs around the windows and upper panels.

WALKWAYS

Walkways run around the gas-holder at a number of levels. On some prototypes these seem to be evenly spaced, while on others, those nearer to the top are closer together. The walkways on the model were constructed using the basic methods outlined in the section on stairways and walkways in Chapter 5. Styrene decking was shaped to follow the polygonal shape of the gas-holder and supported on styrene outriggers fixed to the vertical ribbing. The gas-holder was given a spray with primer at this stage to ensure full coverage before various external details got in the way. The primer also reveals any blemishes, which were attended to with spots of filler or abrasive paper, as required.

Extended-width platforms were added to accommodate the stairway landings, followed by the addition of styrene strip handrails. Finally, Plastruct stairways and styrene handrails linked the various levels. This is another slow process requiring considerable cutting

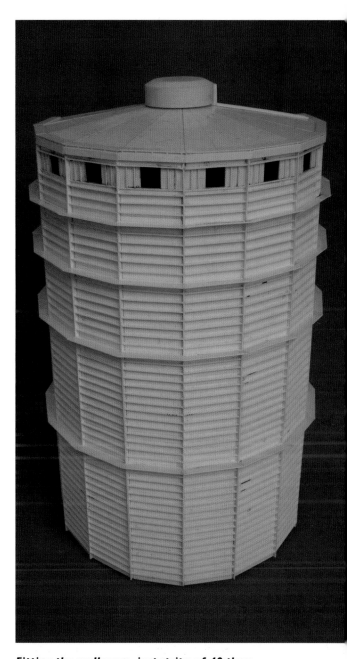

Fitting the walkways, just strips of 40 thou styrene fixed to the horizontal ribs at appropriate spacings.

and fitting but it starts to make a big difference to the look of the model. The final stairway to the roof level was, at this stage, omitted.

On the prototype a few pipes run up the sides of the holder carrying lubricating fluid for the gas seal.

ABOVE: *A coat of primer on the basic tower helps highlight the stairways and handrails.*

On the model these were made from thick, brass wire, detailed with small styrene flanges and held to several ribs by simple styrene brackets.

RIGHT: *The individual roof panels taped on their undersides into a single piece.*

THE ROOF

The roof was constructed from ten segments of styrene, scribed to represent smaller panels. A former of 10mm foamboard provided the 'domed' roof profile with the segments taped together on their undersides, draped over and glued on. A hole or well was left in the centre to accommodate the large, central roof vent.

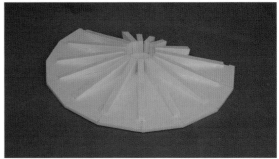

The roof former consists of a base, which sits on the top of the holder, with shallow triangular supports to shape the roof fixed to it.

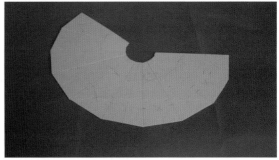

Triangular roof panels. One is needed for each flat side of the holder and the inner ends are cut to leave a round aperture.

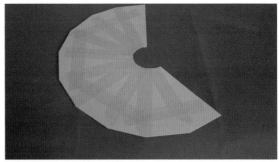

The large, central top vent was made from a number of discs of foamboard; smaller discs make a plug that sits in the well. Fixed on top of this plug were larger diameter discs which form the actual vent. A final smaller disc was glued on the top with a fillet of filler in the shoulder. This was then sanded to represent the sloping edge of the prototype vent.

The various discs were aligned by the simple expedient of pushing a cocktail stick through their centres.

On the real holders, access is required to the space above the internal piston for maintenance and this is provided by a doorway in the side of the central vent. This was built as a simple styrene frame and door. A railed walkway leads from it to the edge of the roof.

Cutting discs of 10mm and 5mm foamboard to form the large central vent.

Basic vent assembly. Card wrapped around covers the exposed foam edges and filler was used to form the sloping shoulder.

The finished vent fitted and detailed with an access doorway.

VENTS

Around the top of the holders stand a number of vertical ventilators. These allow the air above the internal piston to escape as the piston rises. They have a hopper-shaped bottom, a tubular riser and a top rain cap. They were made from styrene sheet and tube, while the rain caps were made from wider tube with a punched disc top.

After painting the hopper bottom of each vent was glued with solvent between the top two ribs of the gas-holder at the appropriate positions. A simple triangular bracket supports them between the mid-points of the vent tube and the gas-holder top. The photographs should make this clear. Two pairs were fitted, spaced out across the top.

That completes the essential structure. It is, without doubt, an imposing model.

GOODS LIFT

A simple elevator is usually provided for easy access to the roof. These run in a panel-clad framework up the side of the gas-holder. The model was simply constructed from an inner core of two lengths of 10mm foamboard glued together and then clad in styrene sheeting.

The styrene was scribed to represent individual panels and the top was cut to represent a peaked roof. Close-up photographs of the exact arrangement proved elusive, so some 'imagineering' was involved. Lift doors and a framework were added at the top and at the base, along with a call-button panel and two indicator lights above the doors.

A small, concrete hoist house built from styrene sits at the base with a steel-panelled hood covering the lifting cables running into the tower.

The steel cladding of the tower was sprayed with Humbrol gunmetal, and details were picked out in appropriate colours. The lift tower stands against the gas-holder, a bracing bracket of H-section styrene holds it at mid-height, and a railed platform links the top of it with the roof.

Making the side vents. Thin styrene wrapped around triangular base formers produced the distinctive hopper shaped bottoms.

With basic assembly complete, the gas-holder was given a coat of primer. At this stage the roof had not been permanently attached to allow access later for fitting the window glazing.

RIGHT: *Parts of the service elevator. The shaft is made from styrene clad foamboard and the hoist mechanism house sits in front.*

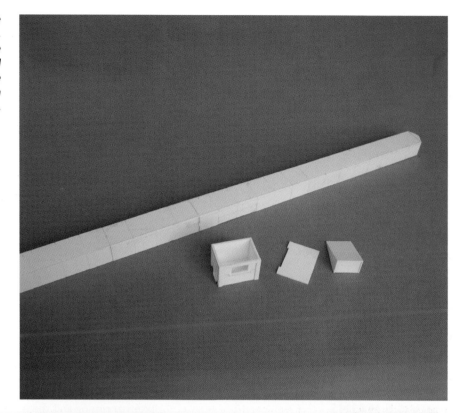

BELOW: *A view of the top of the elevator showing the doors, indicator lights above, and the call button panel.*

The small building housing the hoisting mechanism and the hood housing the cables.

SERVICE MAINS

When the model is finally installed on the layout it will be connected to the coke-oven's gas-cleaning plant and to the works' gas-distribution network. For the time being it sits on its own small baseboard

OIL TANK AND PUMP

As previously mentioned, the seal on these gas-holders is provided by the liberal use of lubricant. A simple oil-tank and pump assembly was built to sit at the base of the gas-holder. The tank was made from 25mm plumbing tube with punched disc ends and the pump cabinet from styrene. The front panel was cut from the louvered bonnet side of a Dapol Drewery shunter kit. This kit will provide louvered doors for other projects along with other bits and pieces.

PAINTING

At this point the gas-holder was given a detailed examination. Any blemishes were tidied up and any gaps filled with plastic filler. This was followed by gentle scrubbing with Cif and a toothbrush, a careful

external rinsing and the holder was then allowed to dry. The main body, the roof and the large, top vent and smaller side vents were separate assemblies at this point. All of the detail, stairways and handrails, had been fitted with the exception of the final stairway leading up to the roof.

A couple of thin coats of grey primer were sprayed on and allowed to dry. An aerosol of a suitable pale blue, obtained from a DIY store, was used to give the finishing coat. A particularly pale shade was chosen to suggest the loss of colour intensity when seeing a large structure from a distance. In fact the original choice was a little too dark; it can be seen in some of the photos later in the build sequence. After much musing, a second aerosol was obtained.

Warning: If the paints contain different solvents, spraying one paint over another risks the original coat bubbling up and ruining the finish. On a metal kit, the whole lot can be stripped back but this gas-holder really is not a model where you would want to do that. A couple of trials were undertaken on scrap plastic, spraying the new paint over a sample of old to check they were compatible.

RIGHT: *A simple fabrication forming the tank containing the sealing lubricant and pumphouse.*

BELOW: *Drawing up the window frames using paint, a bowpen and a guideline grid.*

WINDOWS

The metal-framed windows were made from clear glazing plastic with glazing bars drawn on, using a bowpen. Taping a large sheet of glazing material over a grid drawn on a piece of paper facilitated the production of enough windows, with a few spares.

A small strip of foamboard was glued to the inner gas-holder wall, just beneath each window aper-

ture, for the glazing panel to sit on. The panels were installed behind the window apertures and fixed in place using Klear floor polish as glue, and with some strips of tape around the edge to reinforce the joint. Once the roof is on, these will be inaccessible so they need to be secure. If one drops out it would be difficult to replace.

FINAL ASSEMBLY

The roof was placed in position and the top vent inserted into the well, both held with UHU. The final top stairway and handrails were fitted and, with the windows carefully masked, primed and sprayed blue. Though the method of fitting was mentioned earlier in this chapter, I did not fix the tubular, vertical vents until this point. As they are fixed to both the gas-holder and its roof, I had to wait until the roof was finally in place.

With that, one of the larger projects was complete. It has a real sense of bulk. Standing 150ft/45m tall, it is bigger than some, but smaller than many prototypes. However, if anything, it demonstrates the importance of getting the balance of a model right. Any larger and it would start to look like a model built to a different, larger scale and would overwhelm anything else on the layout.

Most modellers looking at the gas-holder from the Bachmann Scenecraft range would realize straight away that it is under-scale. I doubt that many modellers looking at this model would know or think it small.

ABOVE: *A pair of the small vents fitted to the top of the gas-holder.*

RIGHT: *The completed gas-holder. It will receive some light weathering before its final installation.*

**Bachmann's resin gas-holder, minus some of its detail, stands alongside
the scratchbuilt model. Quite a contrast.**

A SECOND GAS-HOLDER

I have had the Model Power gas-holder in storage for some years now and thought it would make a contrast to the waterless gas-holder. It is a ready-built plastic model, though on inspection it can be seen to have been assembled from several moulded plastic components: a ready assembled kit, essentially.

Taking apart a solvent-assembled kit is not always easy and, owing to the strength of the joints, not without risk of damage. Nonetheless, the two rings of walkways and handrails came away readily enough using a scalpel to part the joints. Being finely moulded they did not have large surface areas to which solvent had been applied.

The external framework was removed by cutting cleanly through the bases of the uprights and then separating the guide brackets, which were very lightly glued to the tank top.

With tank and framework separated, they were cleaned up and primed followed by airbrushing both components with a pale, washed-out green. The upper part of the tank was masked off and the lower section sprayed with Humbrol gunmetal from an aerosol. On the Model Power gas-holder, the lower part of the tank was intended to represent a fixed lower section, i.e. one that does not sink into a water-filled 'pit' below ground-level. In this design the upper levels drop into the base section and, because they are frequently bathed in the water forming the gas-tight seals, they soon develop a coating of rust.

Three shades of rust-effect weathering powders were thickly and vigorously brushed around the mid-portion of the tank leaving just a thin green band at the top, the part that would not dip below the water seal. Some dark-grey streaks were then brushed over the rust powder.

The framework was next slipped back over the tank and secured with a little solvent at the base of each upright. A stairway made up from Plastruct components and styrene strip was fitted at the side of the structure.

The whole model was then weathered using an airbrush and enamel paints followed by removing some of the paint from the sides and framework with a thinners-dampened brush and downward strokes.

The Model Power gas-holder in Gulf colours.

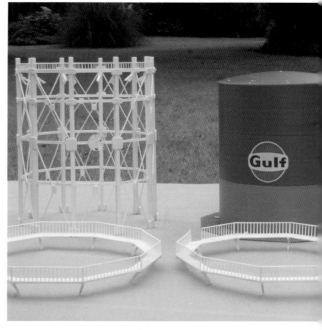

Stripped into its component parts, the ladders and walkways went into the bits box.

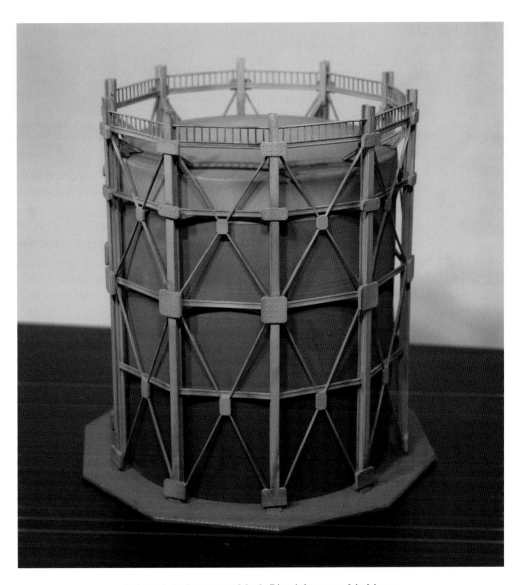

Painted and reassembled. Pity it's not a bit bigger.

CONCLUSION

This chapter has outlined the building of two very different gas-holders. The waterless gas-holder is a very large model and yet still represents a relatively small example of its type. I think that it captures the look of the real thing and it will certainly be a dominant feature when installed on the layout.

The modified Model Power holder is a very nice little model, the components being well detailed and crisply moulded. It is a pity that for its intended scale, 3.5mm/ft, it is so small, as otherwise it is a fine model of a Victorian-style gas-holder, needing just a little extra detailing and repainting into a more workmanlike livery to lift it to another level. If still available, I believe that Gaugemaster intend to reintroduce the model as this book is published, it might offer some interesting possibilities in a 2mm/ft application. My model will eventually see service as a small gas-holder on part of the coke-oven's byproduct plant.

CHAPTER SEVEN

TANK FARM

THE PROTOTYPE

The storage of bulk liquids other than water is a common need for many industries. Examples would be oils used for fuel or oils and chemicals stored pending, or during, a manufacturing process. Storage tanks are generally of steel construction, sometimes concrete, and may be lagged if the contents need some form of heat insulation. The photograph of the tanks at British Steel's Shepcote Lane Works in Sheffield shows oil-storage tanks and the corrugated outer shell suggests that these tanks were lagged.

Some tanks have a short and squat aspect; others are relatively tall and narrow. There seem to be no rules or conventions determining whether tall or squat tanks are used. A small wall built around the foot of the tanks forms a bund – a structure that would contain the contents of the tanks should they suffer a catastrophic leak or rupture. An alternative to a brick or concrete bund wall is the provision of a berm. Where there is plenty of space available, a berm, a raised earthwork ridge, provides the bund. They are often used on large tank farms and around large tanks as they are quick and cheap to form with heavy earthmoving equipment. Such a containment provision is mandatory for tanks containing many liquids, fuels and oils, for example, for both environmental and safety reasons.

The tanks themselves are constructed from pre-cut and pre-shaped steel panels welded together on site. The seams between these individual plates are often very visible, though on many more modern tanks they are almost invisible. External details include access stairways, handrails, inspection hatches and walkways, along with pipework and valves to handle the tank's contents.

Oil storage tanks at the British Steel Corporations Shepcote Lane works in Sheffield. The brick bund is clearly visible as are pipes, stairways and handrails. TATA STEEL EUROPE

Storage tanks at the Lanstar works at Cadishead on the north bank of the Manchester Ship Canal.

THE PROJECT MODEL

My need was for two or three vertical oil-storage tanks, inspired by a rather poor photograph of some tanks serving the No. 2 melting shop at Shotton Steelworks. As with most of British industry, coal, either direct or as coke or gas, was the standard fuel into the 1950s. Open-hearth furnaces had been traditionally fired, largely with producer gas, made from coal. In those early post-war years, as the cost of coal increased, the relative costs of both oil and electricity dropped. As a consequence, most British steelworks turned to oil-firing their open-hearth furnaces with heavy grades of bunker oil. Oil was a more controllable fuel and offered another significant advantage too. Producer gas carried with it a large volume of fine ash. Such was the volume of gas consumed by the open-hearth furnaces that within a few days the ash content blocked the air and gas passageways and reduced efficiency. It was the general practice to run the furnaces from Monday morning to Friday evening and, with the furnaces cooling over the weekend, clear the ash out of the brick chequerwork. Oil-firing reduced the ash problem to virtually zero and overnight the furnaces were making steel seven days a week – a significant increase in the output of the melting shop at little extra cost.

This is a simple project and though kits are available, large storage tanks are readily made from any suitably sized, round item. Walthers have H0 kits available to make two sizes of tank: one described as 'wide' (190mm wide x 100mm tall) and another described as 'tall' (150mm wide x 159mm tall).

THE STORAGE TANKS

The prototype tanks inspiring this model were tall and relatively narrow, so two sections of 60mm plastic pipe 180mm tall and a single section of 75mm plastic pipe 110mm tall were chosen. These were scribed around horizontally and vertically to represent the individual panels from which the tanks are constructed. The smaller tanks were scribed horizontally using a pipe cutter; however, the larger pipe was beyond the capacity of my largest cutter and the seams were scribed using a large jubilee clip.

Using a jubilee clip to scribe horizontal seems around a large plastic pipe.

Making a shallow coned roof by slicing a segment from a disc of styrene. With the cut edges brought together, a cone is formed.

This method works well but is just a little slower than the pipe-cutter method. Both tanks had the horizontal lines scribed at 24mm spacing. The jig that had been constructed to aid construction of the coal-blending plant was used, along with a steel rule, to scribe the vertical seams. These were staggered across the horizontal lines in a 'brickwork' pattern. The tall tanks were scribed into six panels and the wide tank scribed to represent eight panels.

The top of the larger diameter tank is a flattened cone cut from styrene sheet, again scribed to represent panelling. There are online calculators, so search for 'cone calculator', which will indicate the flat shape that needs to be cut to form any size of cone. Flat cones, as used here, need little calculation. A disc slightly larger than the large tank was cut from 30 thou styrene and then a narrow segment cut from that. The cut edges were then drawn together, secured beneath with duct tape, and solvent run down the seam.

This disc was attached to the tank body with a thick bead of plumbing solvent and left to dry. The following day the overlapping edges were sanded back to match the tank body diameter and the joint in the cone improved with Squadron White filler.

Discs of styrene form the tops of the narrow tanks, again scribed to represent panelling. On all three tanks a narrow strip of Evergreen styrene reinforcing band was run around both the top and the bottom. These need to be attached with plumber's solvent, though some solvent can be run around the joints between the top strip and the tank top, both of which are styrene.

STAIRWAYS, WALKWAYS AND TANK DETAILS

The handrail stanchions are 18mm lengths of Slater's 40 thou x 40 thou section and the styrene band around the tank tops allows the use of solvent. The handrails are 30 thou x 20 thou strips and, because they would need to follow the curve of the tank sides, they were pre-formed. Lengths were wrapped around spare bits of tube, held with tape and placed in a warm oven, 100°C is fine. After an hour they were removed and cooled under the tap. This considerably eases the fitting of the handrails as they do not try to spring away as the solvent sets.

Plastruct caged ladders run up the side of one of the tall tanks and the two tank tops are linked with a short footbridge. Storage tanks often feature a stairway that follows the curve of the side. To model this type of stairway, simply remove one side of a set of Plastruct steps with a craft knife. Starting at the

Pre-curving handrails by taping thin styrene strip around off cuts of plastic pipe. An hour in a warm oven does the job.

bottom of the tank, fix the inner edge of the stair, just a few millimetres of it, to the tank with plumber's solvent. I also liberally brush on some modeller's solvent to help the bond.

Leave that to fully cure overnight. When firmly fixed, start to curve the stair up and around the tank. Check that the steps splay out evenly and that the stair climbs at a constant gradient whilst fixing the stair to the tank with plumber's solvent. Masking tape carefully bound around steps and tank will hold it firm until the solvent has set. Leave overnight to be certain that the solvent bond has fully dried. The stairs are completed by adding an outer riser of 30 x 80 thou styrene strip. This method of installing a spiral stairway works down to tanks of 50mm diameter, I have not tried anything smaller, but it does become more difficult as the diameter reduces. The stairway on the wider tank includes a halfway landing.

With the stairway and its outer riser firmly fixed, handrails were built up with the usual styrene sections. The pre-curved styrene strip was used to make up the handrails.

Final details on the tanks started with the fitting of a manhole cover at the base of each tank. These were made from short lengths of 12mm Plastruct tube inserted into a hole drilled into the base of each tank and capped with 13mm-diameter punched styrene discs. Manholes were also added to the top of each

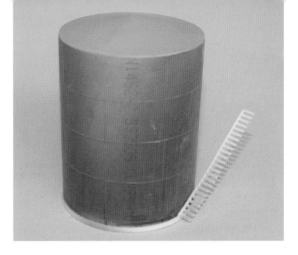

Forming a curved stairway. The Plastruct stairs have had one edge removed and the bottom has been glued to the bottom of the tank and left to set.

The tank showing the lower stairway fitted, a landing in place and masking tape holding the upper stairway to the tank while the solvent sets.

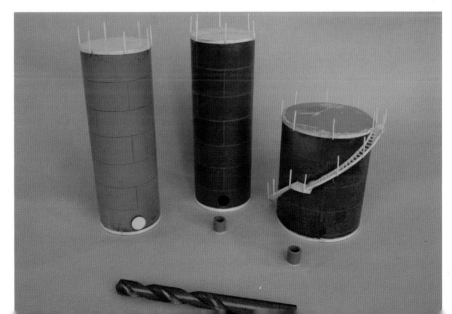

All three tanks partly detailed with handrails and having the manhole covers fitted.

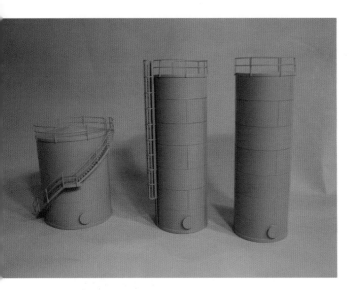

The tanks largely completed and primed.

An aerial view of some storage tanks at Port Talbots by product plant. There is some useful detail visible in the photograph and note the rail tank wagon just visible top left. TATA STEEL EUROPE

tank and these are simply made from two discs of styrene, a larger disc sitting on top of a smaller one.

Each of the tall tanks was fitted with a vent pipe. These are lengths of 2mm brass wire, curved over at the top, and with short lengths of styrene tube fitted at each end to represent fittings at the top and bottom. Lights were added from 0.7mm brass wire with Grandt Line lamp fittings and bulbs added from clear beads.

After priming and tidying up, all three tanks were sprayed with matt black paint from an aerosol.

THE BUND AND OIL-HANDLING EQUIPMENT

The tanks sit on a concrete base that was made up from foamboard to which a piece of 120 grit abrasive paper was glued with PVA. The bund walls are strips of 5mm foamboard clad with embossed styrene brickwork. Though pedestrian access into the bund will be by a small footbridge, there is a fluid-tight, steel door, a simple styrene fabrication, to allow heavier objects to be moved in and out but which would otherwise be kept firmly shut. The footbridge comprises a top walkway accessed with lengths of Plastruct styrene steps and supported on a frame-work made from Evergreen sections. Lighting again is provided by Grandt Line fittings and brass wire.

A kit from Knightwing provided a rail tank unloading facility. I believe that, as with some other Knightwing kits, this is a repackaged Walthers kit. It provides a walkway, pipework, valves and flexible hoses, along with other details. I cut sections out of the walkway and rejoined them so that each unloading point was spaced to match the lengths of 14-ton railway tank wagons. The unloading rack is long enough to accommodate six such oil-tank wagons. Each unloading stand is illuminated by a floodlight made from 2mm plastic rod drilled to accept a shaped 0.7mm wire head with a Grandt Line shade.

The Knightwing kits come with a length of 2mm-diameter rubber tube to make up the flexible hoses that would be attached to the rail tank wagons. I thought that, once cut into six, each length would be a little short, so I bought some 2mm rubber tube that is sold for jewellery use and made up some longer lengths and some spares to help detail the scene. Screw couplings on the end of each length are represented by 2mm lengths of styrene tube painted a brass colour.

A small pumphouse was constructed from styrene, clad in styrene brick sheet and fitted with a simple concrete slab roof.

The completed model showing the bund wall and some detail of the unloading rack.

A view of the pumphouse and some of the pipework, with the fire-fighting trolley visible by the front wall.

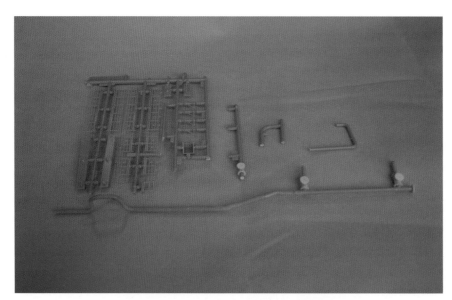

A section of the pipework under construction. This length was made from scrap kit sprue with scratchbuilt valves.

A short rake of tank wagons being positioned by one of the works'
diesel shunters. The fire fighting trolley sits by the pumphouse.

The completed tank farm.

To fill the internal void, a 'pump' was quickly assembled from some plastic oddments and sprayed pale blue. A simple instrument panel was also made up from styrene, painted black and with some white dials painted on.

Final details were the addition of three oil drums standing against the bund wall and a fire-fighting trolley that stands outside the pumphouse. The trolley itself has a rear frame made from a spare bit of Scalelink window etching, a styrene base and punched styrene wheels. The bottles are white-metal castings and their hoses looped up from some elastic filament.

Pipework construction has its own section in Chapter 5. For this project, pipes run on ground-level racks from the unloading stands, pairing up before running through valves, into a single manifold and then into the pumphouse. A second run leaves the pumphouse, loops up over the bund wall, runs behind the tanks and feeds, through valves and vertical pipes, each tank in turn. Finally, a return pipe runs from the base of each tank, over the wall and back into the pumphouse. On the completed model, a pipeline will run from the tank farm over to the melting shop, its final positioning yet to be determined.

PAINTING AND WEATHERING

Weathering started by airbrushing the grime and rust/oxide mix over the tanks and pipework, just varying the intensity on individual surfaces and wiping some off with downward strokes from a paintbrush.

As these tanks will serve, and be located close by, the melting shop they would be subject to a constant sprinkling of iron oxide laden dust from the furnace chimneys. The tops have a thin spray of rust-coloured paint to represent this. This has been restrained as the level of covering seen in reality would look over-done on a model. Oil spills and leaks were added around valves, pipe joints and hoses using a brush and a mix of semi-matt black with a splash of brown. The tank bodies were highlighted by brushing on weathering powders. A 'steel' powder gives an oily, grey sheen and a mix of this with a little rust-coloured powder highlighted the seam lines. The track and adjacent areas have a spray of the black brown oil mix to suggest the oil spills and dribbles of several years use.

CONCLUSION

Though this is a small tank farm, the techniques used are applicable to any size and any number of storage tanks. The provision of ladders, walkways, bunds and pipework would be exactly the same. The challenge would be to find cylindrical objects of the right size to represent whatever sized prototypes are being modelled. Making up and fitting pipe runs can be quite time-consuming but it does add a lot of interest to the model. It's a task that can be divided into sections. I assembled and fitted one pipe run, left it for a few days before making up another, and so on.

CHAPTER EIGHT

OVERHEAD TRAVELLING CRANES

INTRODUCTION

Overhead cranes running on rails are a very common feature of heavy industry. They most usually, though not always, operate within the confines of a building. Those operating outside are an interesting feature and often serve a rail siding. There are a number of detail differences between various cranes but the common feature is an overhead lifting mechanism that can be moved both along the bay served, and across it, allowing lifting at any point under the crane.

SOME PROTOTYPES

Internally operating cranes run on rails mounted on, and supported by, the structure of the building they serve. Clearly, the original structure will have

been designed with this in mind. External cranes will run on rails and heavy steel beams supported on steel towers of some sort. The first photograph shows a crane operating at Trostre Works in Llanelli. It is typical of the type of general crane operating at many facilities. In fact, in the lifting operation featured, there is a second identical crane sharing the same tracks and positioned immediately behind the first crane. The two are working in tandem, each lifting one end of the spreader beam to enable them to lift the mill housing off the railway wagon. The housing weighs something approaching 100 tons, the cranes themselves having a 50-ton maximum lift on their main hoists. Large cranes, like these, might also have a light-capacity, supplementary hoisting mechanism too. Very high lifting capacity mechanisms operate slowly and it is often convenient to have a smaller,

50-ton capacity overhead travelling crane at Trostre Steelworks in South Wales TATA STEEL EUROPE

An outdoor crane serving a steel stock yard in Sheffield.
TATA STEEL EUROPE

yet quicker, mechanism for lighter jobs. The sign on the crane at Trostre indicates that it has a 50-ton main hoist and an auxiliary hoist of 10-ton capacity.

A variant of this arrangement has one rail supported on the outside of a building, the crane serving a bay running adjacent to and parallel to it. The other rail could run at the same level being supported on vertical members or, as shown in the photograph, at ground-level with the crane having its own support structure at that end. The crane in the photograph serves a steel coil stockyard in Sheffield.

These types of cranes can be used to move materials and work pieces, locomotives, e.g. about an engineering shop or finished goods in stockyards and loading bays.

The long travel, that is the movement along the rails, is limited only by the space available and length of the rails, whereas the cross-travel, the distance

Open-hearth melting shop crane moving a teeming ladle at Appleby Frodingham Steelworks in Scunthorpe. TATA STEEL EUROPE

A specialized soaking-pit crane also working at Appleby Frodingham Steelworks. TATA STEEL EUROPE

between the rails, has limits imposed by the strength of the crane girders. For any given weight-lifting capacity, these girders need to be ever-more substantial as the width increases. Such cranes are available in a very wide range of capacities, ranging from a few tons to several hundreds of tons and increased capacity is reflected in the ever greater aspect of the components. The cross-girders that form the bridge are of a number of types. Lattice or truss girders, plate girders or box section girders are all utilized, and they may be underslung from the main rails or ride above them.

The actual lifting mechanism is housed on a trolley or crab that runs on rails across the crane girders. The crab will house the electric hoist motors, winches, gearing and control mechanisms. Usually the lifting cables drop between the main girders, though on some they drop down on either side. The photograph of the ladle crane shows some of these features and, in particular, the lifting mechanism on the trolley and the low-slung driver's cab. This is a 125-ton capacity

Wellman ladle crane that once served the Appleby melting shop in Scunthorpe.

Larger cranes usually have a driver's cab, supported at one end of the cross-girders and travelling up and down with the crane. This positioning provides the driver with a good view of the work area below. On some specialized cranes, e.g. steelworks' soaking-pit cranes, the driver's cab hangs from the trolley and travels crossways with it. With this arrangement the driver has an even better view, looking right down at the lifting-point and load. The soaking-pit crane illustrated is seen withdrawing an incandescent ingot from a soaking pit from where it will be transferred to the rolling mill. Rather than a simple cross-trolley it has a complex machinery structure hanging from the bridge, housing control equipment and the machinery to operate the gripping mechanism. For obvious reasons the crane must be able to grasp the load, between its tongs, unassisted, so it is essential for the driver to have a good view of operations. These cranes also transfer cold ingots from storage into the soaking pits and very similar cranes are used to strip ingot moulds off the ingots earlier in the process. In the open-hearth melting shop build (Chapter 14), cranes of this type would operate in the stripping and mould preparation bay.

Smaller cranes might be operated from the ground with a control pendant hanging on a cable from the bridge. Today radio control is also widely used. A specialized crane of this type is the ore bridge. This is a very large crane spanning a wide ore or minerals' stockyard, which utilizes a clam-shell bucket to move materials to and fro. These stockyards may be adjacent to a wharf or dock, the ore bridge being used to unload the bulk ore carriers too.

THE PROJECT MODEL

The model represents one of the larger examples of overhead crane that would be found outside and the prototype photograph shows a crane installed at Port Talbot Steelworks. The photograph is included at the end of this chapter to better facilitate a comparison between the prototype and the model. The job of this crane was to break up both lumps of cold slag and large scrap iron and steel castings to make the latter more suitable for recycling in the furnaces. In the photograph a large steel ball, weighing several tons, can be seen dropping away from the crane's lifting magnet and about to drop on, and break up, something below. This particular crane has long travel rails at two levels. On the high-level rails runs one crane equipped with the magnet and breaking ball. This can be seen clearly closest to the camera. Further back, running on the lower rails, are two lighter cranes that are equipped with grabs with which they clear the broken materials. An unusual feature is the large stair tower giving access to the cabs of the cranes; a caged ladder usually suffices. A stair tower, as fitted to the prototype on which this model is based, is quite a complex structure. It could be replaced by a caged ladder or straight stairway, both of which are much easier to build. I had a stair tower available from a Walthers detailing kit, which was built up to serve the crane. Unfortunately, it proved to be undersized and I will replace it with a scratch-built tower at a future date.

THE MAIN SUPPORT GIRDERS

The long-travel girders were fabricated from styrene sheet and strip. They are supported on fabricated plate girders made up from Central Valley parts. Central Valley are a US manufacturer who make and sell a range of railroad bridges and they sell the girders and structural members separately. In the absence of kit parts, the uprights could be fabricated from sheet and strip, from Evergreen sections or Plastruct truss girders.

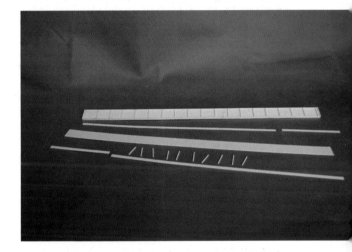

The components for making up the long travel support girders and, at the top, a completed girder.

The vertical support girders made up from Central Valley kit components with styrene support saddles at the top ends.

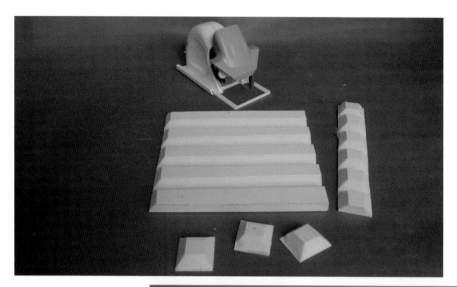

Cutting out the concrete support pads from foamboard using the Foamwerks 'V' cutter.

The pads, painted with tinted masonry paint, fitted to the base board.

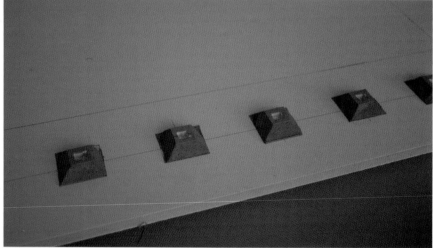

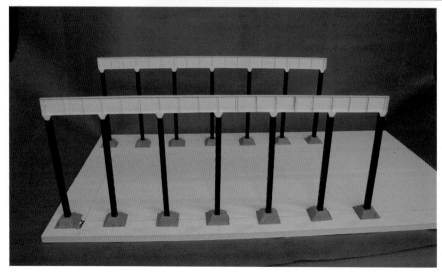

The crane support girders erected on the baseboard.

Strengthening plates were cut from 40 thou styrene to reinforce the upright to long-girder joints. The NWSL Chopper, with its guides set appropriately, was used to cut consistent shapes. Concrete bases for the support members were cut from 10mm foamboard using a Foamwerk's V cutter. Looking something like a mechanical bird or preying insect, it uses two angled blades to remove a V-shaped groove from the board. By cutting lengthways and then crosswise, a chocolate-block effect is created. These taper-sided blocks are then cut free and provide suitably shaped bases.

The V cutter generally cuts cleanly but when used for cross-cutting, as it emerges into open grooves, the unsupported foam edge does tend to tear a little. This was of no concern as the bottom edges of the blocks will be lost in ground cover and in real life they would get lumps knocked out of their corners. These blocks were fixed to the base in two lines, spaced apart to correspond with the crane's girders. Small, square holes cut into these blocks with a scalpel allowed the upright girders to be inserted into them, where they were fixed with UHU. Squares and rulers ensured that both sides were level, upright and square, before the glue hardened.

With short lengths of I-section styrene forming saddles, the long girder sits on the uprights with the previously cut strengtheners fitted on either side. The two matching assemblies were then erected with the uprights glued into the foamboard blocks. Lengths of code 75 rail, on which the crane runs, were fixed to styrene strips and fitted along the tops of the long girders. Stop blocks, fitted later, were made up from square section and sheet styrene, and sit at each end of the rail, preventing what could otherwise be a rather catastrophic accident.

Vertical outriggers fitted to one side, and standing off a little way, support four longitudinal busbars or contact rails, which provide electrical power to the crane as it moves along. The four busbars are lengths of Slater's 40 x 40 thou strip and they sit on tiny discs punched from 40 thou sheet with a leather punch. These discs represent the insulators and they are fixed to brackets made up from I-channel strip. An electrical cabinet sits at the bottom of one of the end uprights, which would contain the switchgear, controlling power to the crane. It is made from styrene sheet and a length of square-section tube representing cable-ducting runs up to the busbars.

Taken much later in the construction process, this photograph shows the electrical busbars and collector shoes from which the crane collects power as it moves along.

Electrical control cabinet with the ducting carrying the cables leading off to the right and up one of the support columns.

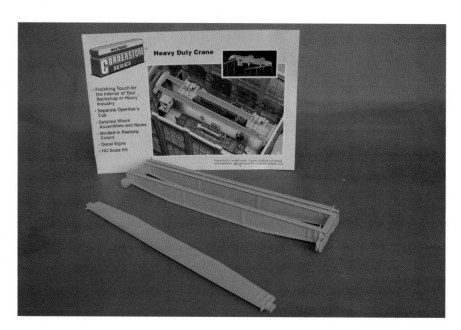

The Walthers heavy-duty crane and the crane bridge made up from two Walthers kits.

THE CRANE BRIDGE

The crane itself utilizes parts from two Walthers heavy-duty crane kits, the second kit providing a second set of main girders. This might seem a little wasteful but the remaining parts will see use on subsequent crane builds, using sets of shorter girders fabricated from styrene.

The second set of girders was used to create a more massive crane by doubling up on the cross-members. In the photographs that follow, any Walthers parts are yellow, while all the scratchbuilt parts are white. The girders and end trolleys from the Walthers kit were assembled using solvent and they provided a strong and square framework on which further construction could continue using styrene sheet and section. An access platform was constructed around the top of the girders supported on T-section angles.

Beneath this platform, using styrene sections and filler, a number of detailing components were added. A drive motor for the long travel, a main gearbox linked to gearboxes on the end trolleys with a drive shaft, and mechanical lubricators for the wheel bearings were all fabricated and then fitted. White-metal buffers from the spares' box were fitted at both ends and both sides of the crane girders. These were installed to line up with

stop blocks fitted at the end of the long-travel girders. A small triangular framework holds the contact shoes, which run along the busbars and collect electric power. On top of the walkways, electrical equipment cabinets and an air reservoir sit, all made from styrene. The domed ends of the air tanks are simply blobs of Squadron White filler sanded to shape.

The cab is largely that from the Walthers kit. The lower cab front was angled back to provide a better view for the driver and the moulded-on cab door sanded off, with a new one suggested at the back with a simple styrene frame. A larger floor was added, supported on H-section strip, and a support framework fitted to the roof. The larger floor allows a walkway at the side and rear of the cab, which provides a link to the access stairway from the ground, and from which stairs lead up to the top walkway. The whole cab assembly was then suspended beneath the crane girders at one end. Side windows and the large front window were fitted after painting. They comprise Scalelink-etched frames with clear acetate glazing attached using Klear floor polish.

Such a large and costly plant would work 24h a day and ample flood lighting would be provided under the crane bridge. The Grandt Lines' parts used

The bridge with extra detail added in white styrene.

A close-up showing some of the added detail and the white metal loco buffers fitted.

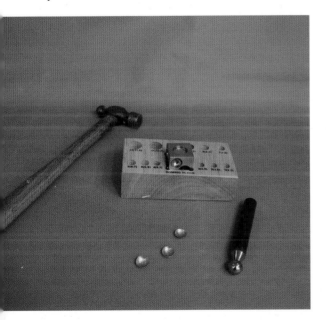

Using the doming block to make dished light shades from brass discs.

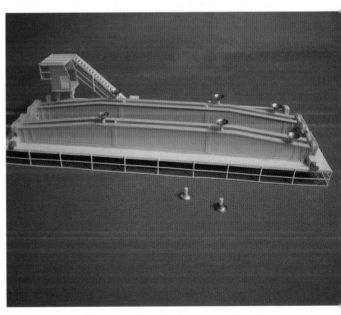

The lamps, fitted with styrene tube housings, being mounted under the crane bridge.

on other projects would be too small, so some were fabricated. Discs of thin brass, 12mm in diameter, were punched out and then domed using a jeweller's doming block.

Short lengths of styrene tube superglued on top provide a lamp body. The completed lamps, eight in number, were glued under the bridge. After painting, light bulbs were added from 2mm clear beads.

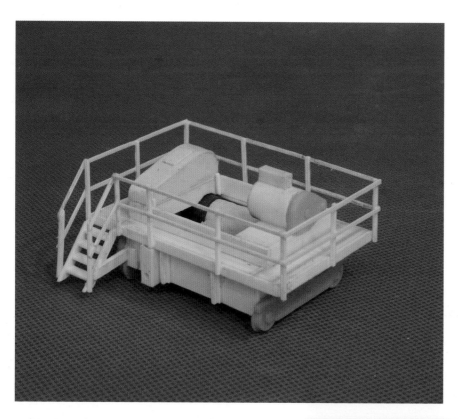

A view of the cross-travel trolley.

THE CROSS-TRAVEL TROLLEY

The cross-travel trolley is based on Walthers kit parts. Only the sides, with their moulded-on wheels, were used after some of the other detailing had been removed. The structure consists of a box assembled with the Walthers side-frames on either side. Within these sit two winch drums made up from tube and wrapped with a grey thread, simulating the lifting cables.

An access platform, with handrails and a short stairway, runs around the top. One of the details carved off the original Walthers side was fixed to a length of styrene tube and, with a few other details added, became an electric motor. This sits on one side, above the winches. On the other side, a gear-box-cover made from styrene sheet, and detailed with punched discs and ribs, covers the ends of the winches.

Code 75 rails provide a running surface for the trolley fitted with stop blocks at either end. The gauge was set using a simple notched styrene jig.

It is common practice for the trolley to be supplied with power via a heavy cable suspended

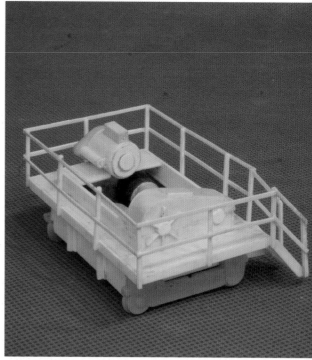

A view from the other side.

The trolley sitting on the bridge. Rails for the trolley have been fitted, setting the gauge with the simple notched styrene strip on the right.

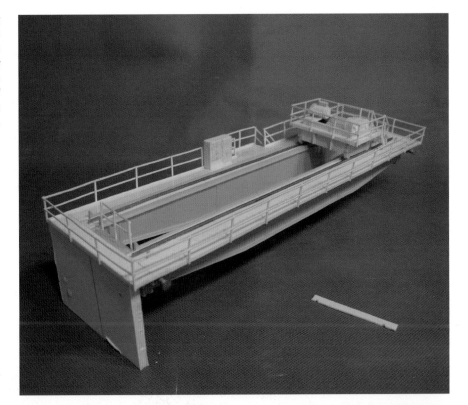

Making up the heavy cable using low-melt solder and a simple jig.

The heavy cable hanging in loops from its support rail and linking the bridge to the trolley.

from, and able to slide along, a rail. As the trolley moves, the cable stretches out behind it and loops back as it returns. Trying to replicate the way heavy cable hangs on the prototype was a challenge. The type of wire used by modellers, if looped, does not hang in the same way. The solution was to use a length of low-melt solder wire, which, being soft and pliable, could be folded to look like a heavy cable hanging in loops. A simple jig made from fine pins and a block of wood was used to form the cable.

A rod of styrene runs between the crane ends and the solder 'cable' hangs from this on 5mm split rings. One end of the cable fits into a junction box on the crane end-frame, the other into a junction box on the trolley.

THE MAGNET AND BREAKER BALL

The lifting hook is that provided in the Walthers kit and is suspended from the winch drums on the

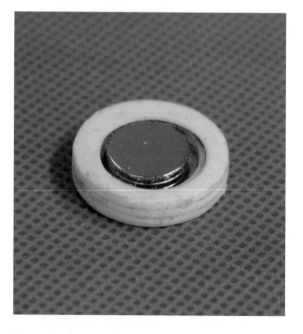

A neodymium magnet sitting in a styrene outer casing made up from punched discs.

trolley by four runs of grey thread. A large ball-bearing provided the breaking ball and, being steel, it was decided to use a magnet to hold it. Three 20mm discs were punched from 40 thou styrene, and then punched into rings with 12mm centre holes and then cemented together. A bottom disc was punched from 15 thou styrene and fixed to the bottom. Three 10 x 1mm neodymium magnets sit in the well, held with UHU, and two 18mm discs fixed on top hold them in place.

The lifting magnet was completed by filing flutes around the top corners. Three lifting lugs, made from brass wire, were fitted on the top along with an electrical connection made from styrene tube. Three small lengths of chain run from the lifting lugs to a split ring, which can be located on the crane's lifting hook. The magnet within is more than capable of holding the rather heavy ball-bearing, which in turn provides tension on the crane's lifting cables, keeping them nice and taut.

FINISHING

Both bridge and trolley were cleaned using water, a domestic cleaner and an old toothbrush. Once dry, both parts were given two thin coats of grey car primer. An industrial-looking washed-out green was then airbrushed over the entire construction. Weathering included grease and oil staining on hubs, bearings and drive shaft housings. The masking tape around the winch cables was removed and some graphite powder brushed on to them. This gives a shiny, greased look to the cable.

GROUND DETAILS

Dropping a large steel ball on to metal castings results in bits flying off like shrapnel and a concrete-lined pit is usually provided to contain this hazard. A square hole, 60 x 60mm, was cut into the foamboard base and a box, constructed from 5mm foamboard, was glued to the underside. To replicate the thick concrete walls of the prototype pit, a second box, sized to fit inside the foamboard box, was made up from 40 thou styrene sheet. A flat styrene rim, 10mm wide, was then fitted around the top. The insides of this box were pitted and scarred using various metal

The concrete pit made up from styrene, heavily distressed and ready to fit into the baseboard.

The pit in place surrounded by the heavy protective steel screens. Some broken ingot moulds lie nearby.

Making ladle-shaped slag lumps by casting a mix of DIY filler and pointing mortar in RT Models' slag ladle bodies.

implements and a burr in a mini-drill to suggest the damage done by the flying metal shards. This was then given a concrete finish and heavily weathered with rust and grime.

Some of the metal components broken up would be oily or greasy and this would become spattered on the sides and bottom. Steel plate screens made from 60 thou styrene supported on styrene frames sit around the top of the breaking pit providing further protection; these too were distressed to replicate damage. Their lifting hooks are thin slivers of tube cut in half and then cemented to the top.

Two rail lines run under the crane: one a though line and one terminated with a stop block. Ground cover is dry pointing mortar sprinkled over a coating of PVA glue, used as a basic ground-cover on most of these projects. A roadway of hard-packed 'slag' runs

under the crane from one end so that the broken slag can be returned to the slag-processing plant in large off-road tippers. Larger pieces of crushed mortar, formed into piles, represent the cold slag being worked on under the crane. Some of this mortar was cast into RT Models and Walthers slag ladle bodies. Slag allowed to cool in ladles came out in solid lumps and required breaking prior to further processing. These ladle-shaped lumps of slag were sometimes used as large road cones and for other purposes. One here provides the stop block on the siding. Four life-expired ingot moulds, high-quality iron castings in reality, sit broken and await further breaking. These resin models are from the RT Models' range, broken up with pliers for the purpose. A variety of interesting plastic and metal shapes represent the large castings that the crane would be breaking up.

The breaker ball, a ball bearing, hangs from the magnet under the crane.

A view under the crane with mineral wagons and slag ladles standing on the sidings.

Looking along the crane to compare with the prototype photograph.

The crane at Port Talbot, which provided inspiration for the model. TATA STEEL EUROPE

Starting another model crane using Peco N gauge truss bridge girders and a Walthers crane kit.

I may well extend the crane track when it is installed on the layout and also add that second-level crane track seen on the prototype.

The finished model was photographed from a similar angle to that of the prototype for comparative purposes. The model was not intended to be an exact replica, but to capture its essence. You can judge for yourself how well I have succeeded.

CONCLUSION

The crane project is a good example of a build progressing with a good number of photographs, but without full information of all of the details. Had I waited until full details were available, the build would never have started, let alone have been finished. Some of these details are consolidated from

different prototypes, others are 'imagineered' and are, hopefully, credible solutions. Though a few kit parts were used, this just saved time. In their absence I would have just fabricated suitable parts from styrene and brass.

This is the first of four overhead travelling cranes, plus an ore bridge, to be featured on the main project. The other three, a smaller scrap-yard crane, a heavy, short-span, hot metal crane and a specialized soaking-pit crane, have different features but they will be built using similar techniques. The ore bridge will be largely based on a Walthers kit.

As an example of future plans, the lightest of these cranes, the scrap-yard crane, will utilize Peco N scale truss-girder bridge sides, along with parts of a Walthers light overhead crane kit.

I've made a start.

CHAPTER NINE

SMALL BUILDINGS

INTRODUCTION

Lost amongst the towering chimneys and cavernous sheds, a whole host of small structures will be found scattered about any site of heavy industry. There may well be more small buildings on the site than large ones, though they will account for little of the used space. They will provide accommodation for a whole range of services and functions. Some of these services will be required at most sites, irrespective of the type of industry, e.g. a gatehouse, whilst others would be more industry-specific, e.g. a laboratory.

A non-exclusive list of these types of buildings would include: a gatehouse, a security lodge, canteens, mess rooms, departmental offices or workshops, garages, first-aid posts, ambulance station, works' fire-brigade, weighbridge, machinery house, site offices, training centre, laboratory and so on. The style of buildings housing these functions will vary considerably from simple wooden sheds, possibly housing a contractor's office, through to large and stylish brick-built structures. Modern industry tends to house some of these services in the ubiquitous mobile office, a Portacabin type of structure. Examination of some of the prototype photographs in this book will reveal several such facilities.

The provision of some small buildings is not just prototypical, but adds variety and makes a change from construction buildings on the grand scale.

In this chapter on small buildings I'll describe the modelling of some small structures. Some have origins as ready-made resin buildings, one is a modified kit and the others were built from scratch.

A SITE OR CONTRACTOR'S OFFICE

This is undoubtedly the simplest project described in this book. I have photographs from the 1950s showing temporary office facilities erected at various

The quickest project in this book – a simple modification of a Bachmann resin building.

sites for the contractors engaged in rebuilding works. These buildings were large, sectional wooden buildings, little more than well-built, over-sized, garden sheds. Today's mobile offices, Portacabins, are the standard structure for such use.

I provided such accommodation on the Staplegrove module, set in the 1970s, using a site office in resin from the Bachmann Scenecraft range.

Prior to installation a few modifications were carried out on the building as bought. The door was moved to the opposite end. The new door comprises simply a frame of styrene strip stuck on the surface with the wall within painted as a door. Some steps were fabricated to serve the door, and I printed out a name board in the name of a former steel industry contractor, Davy Ashmores, and applied it to the outer wall. A quick repaint completed the project and it was placed outside the rolling mill building. Two of the contractor's employees stand outside, consulting a large plan.

PUMPHOUSES

Many industries have the need to pump liquids around their site: water, oils, fuels, etc. and the pumps to facilitate this will need some form of housing.

I've used another Bachmann Scenecraft resin building: the generator/boiler house, to build two pumphouses: one on the Staplegrove module and one to serve the large cooling tower.

The Staplegrove pumphouse was modified by cutting off the odd projection on the roof using a fine pull saw and replacing it with a flat, slab roof. This was made up from several layers of thick styrene sheet, which was then covered with 240 grit abrasive paper.

Once painted with Tamiya acrylic buff paint, a simple concrete effect is achieved. The original etched window-frame was removed, repainted and replaced, and a noticeboard, fabricated from styrene and clear sheet, added to the front wall. Some pipework was fabricated from Knightwing components; this emerges from the end-wall and then disappears into underground ducting. After repainting, the final touch was the addition of a 'painted' wall sign, using a homemade decal, identifying the building as the 'No. 1 EAF Pumphouse' (electric arc furnace). As the door is close by a railway track, a short length of safety railing prevents the unwary or the preoccupied making a fatal error.

The second pumphouse conversion from the Scenecraft boiler house has had the roof replaced in exactly the same manner.

The nicely etched window-frames have again been retained and by cutting a section out of the front wall, a roller shutter door was fitted.

Mannesmann pumphouse at the Richard Thomas and Baldwin Landore foundry; plenty of interesting background detail too.
TATA STEEL EUROPE

Unmodified Bachmann generator/boiler house resin building.

Simple modifications turned it into the No. 1 EAF pumphouse on the Staplegrove module.

Removing the raised roof section with a pull saw.

The raised roof section removed with the replacement roof parts awaiting fitting.

With roller shutter door fitted the model sits by the cooling tower.

The tank farm pumphouse showing the purely representational interior detail, it just fills the inner void with something.

The pumphouse in place on the tank farm. The Scalelink window frames are a useful source of industrial windows.

A third pumphouse, this one to serve the needs of the oil-tank farm, was a simple scratchbuild in styrene, brick-effect plastic sheet with window frames cut from a Scalelink etch. A simple interior was fabricated and fitted as outlined in Chapter 7.

WORKS LABORATORY

THE PROTOTYPE

Not all industries would require the services of a dedicated works laboratory. Those that might, include chemical and petroleum works, coke ovens, food-processing plants and any large concern carrying out its own research. The laboratory and office block shown in the accompanying photograph, re-roofed in recent years, still stands and serves the tar distillation plant at Cadishead.

Steelworks had laboratories to carry out, amongst other duties, analysis of steel sampled from the open-hearth furnaces during the heat. This provided information to enable the furnace crew to make any

A works laboratory and office block serving the Lanstar plant at Cadishead west of Manchester.

additions required to bring the steel to specification. Shotton's melting shop was linked to the laboratory with a Lamson tube system. This was a device once commonly used in banks and department stores to move cash around. The item to be moved is placed in a special cartridge, the cartridge inserted into the tube system and compressed air drives it on to its destination. The one at Shotton was out of use for some of the time I worked there. I spent a couple of night shifts as mill runner, taking the still-warm steel samples from the different furnaces, placed in Lamson System cartridges, on foot to the laboratory. I thought I should include a laboratory on my model steelworks.

THE MODEL

I based the laboratory on the Walthers industry office kit.

This builds up into a generic flat-roofed, brick structure with metal-framed windows. As with all Walthers kits, it goes together very well. I had the idea of modifying the building to include a basement with a front 'well' accessed by stairs at the side.

Having assembled the basic kit, a basement front was added from 40 thou styrene and clad in brick effect sheet. A rectangle of styrene formed the base of the well at the front. I removed the extended corners of the parapet walls, extending the coping with styrene section; it shows white in the photograph.

The walls were next painted and weathered, and the window frames, painted in pale green, were installed. As with some of the other projects, a Faller footbridge kit provided a set of steps, which were installed at one side of the building.

With the steps installed, the well in front of the basement was completed. It has styrene walls clad on the inside with brick-effect sheet. This was pre-painted and weathered prior to fitting. The Faller kit also provided some steps to bridge the well and give access to the building's doors.

The base for the building required a sunken pit to accommodate the basement. This was formed by

RIGHT: *The Walthers kit parts are in tan, with my basement addition in brick.*

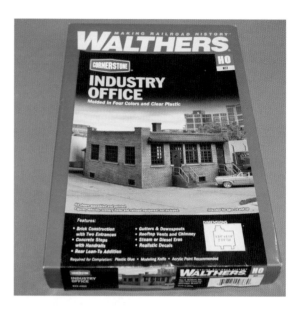

The Walthers industry office kit.

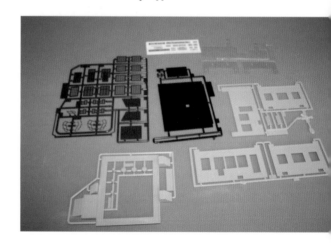

The kit components.

Now painted with the windows fitted and a stairway leading down to the basement level.

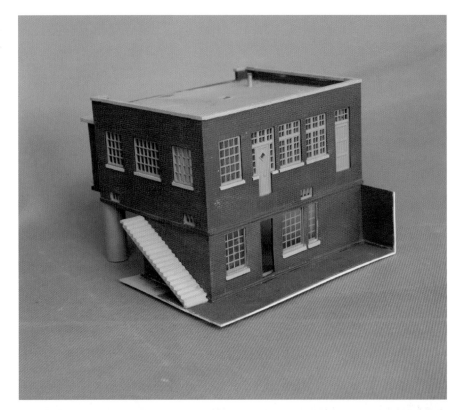

The basement 'well' walled in and steps to form bridges to the doors under construction.

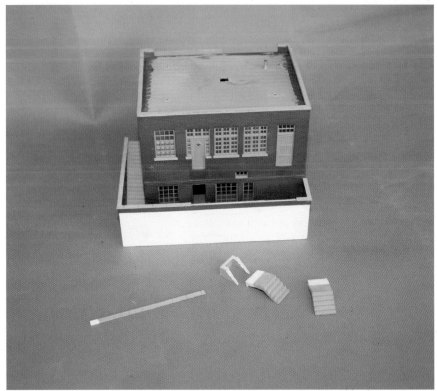

The laboratory base with a well cut into it to accommodate the basement section of the building.

Trial fitting of the laboratory into the well with a dwarf wall and handrails fitted.

RIGHT: *A view from the rear showing the yard, vent detail on the roof, and concrete post and panel fencing erected.*

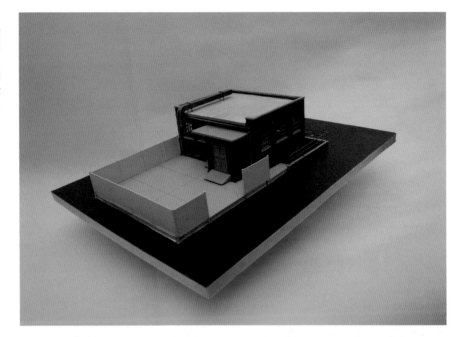

BELOW: *Looking across the rear yard showing the concrete fencing and some of the details inside.*

Peco Modelscene acid carboys with the heavily moulded baskets
removed and wire baskets drawn onto the sides.

The front of the completed laboratory, with a roadway at the side and a rail line running across the front.

Another view of the laboratory front; fire alarm above the right hand door.

cutting an aperture into the foamboard and building a sunken 'box' on the underside.

Construction of the laboratory continued with the completion of a dwarf wall along the edge of the well, the installation of the bridge stairs and handrails from styrene strip. A piece of foamboard provided a concrete slab for the yard at the rear of the building.

This rear yard was provided with a post and panel concrete fence, the construction of which is described in Chapter 4.

Other details include shaded lamps over the door, and stairways and guttering at the rear of the sloping slab roof. I added a large fume extractor with ducting leading out over the roof made up from components included in a Walthers caged ladder kit. Over one

of the front doors I added a fire alarm – a simple assembly made from two punched discs for the bells and a square of styrene as the mechanism.

The laboratory rear yard was detailed by adding some gas cylinders in racks. Some cylinders were made up from styrene rod and others were bought as white metal castings. Some 45gal (205ltr) drums stand along the rear wall. A secure metal cabinet standing on legs sits in one corner with a packing crate over by the far wall. I bought some acid carboys from the Peco range. They are nicely made but the cage around them is very heavy, nothing like the wire cage it is intended to represent. I removed them and drew on the cage with a very fine marker pen.

WORKS CANTEEN

THE PROTOTYPE

Large industrial facilities will almost universally provide catering facilities for staff. Leaving a large facility for offsite food is not practical in terms of time available, so employees will either bring in food or buy it at the canteen.

The two prototype photographs show the then newly built staff and works canteens at Irlam Steelworks in 1955. They are very typical of the flat-roofed, brick-built, metal window-framed buildings erected for all sorts of purposes at the time.

Quite what the differences were between the staff and works canteens I don't know. I can vouch for the very excellent, subsidized, cooked full breakfast in the works canteen at Lancashire Steel. Seriously, one concern was that office staff in suits or flannels would not want to use a chair just vacated by someone wearing greasy overalls.

On some very large sites there might be two or three canteens situated to reduce the walking time between them and the work stations. Canteen facilities might be provided within a central office block or in prefabricated buildings of some description. Today, Portacabin-type structures might provide somewhere for employees to eat food, but not actually provide it.

Lancashire Steel's staff canteen shortly after completion in 1955. A typical flat-roofed, brick-built industrial structure of the time. TATA STEEL EUROPE

The works canteen also newly completed in 1955. The proximity of railway lines is clear and three slag ladle bodies sit in the foreground. TATA STEEL EUROPE

CANTEEN MODEL

The village hall from Hornby's Skaledale range might seem an odd choice for an industrial building. It had a certain look about it, along with an interesting shape that suggested, with some small modifications, it might make a serviceable works canteen. My initial thoughts were that as a wood-clad building, it would represent a short-term structure, perhaps a utility construction surviving from the war years or as a stopgap building pending a larger development. It was difficult to decide quite what sort of material the model's roof was intended to represent.

Playing around with some modelling materials, the option of Wills asbestos sheeting for the roof looked right and this led to thoughts of abandoning the wooden cladding and covering the side-walls with brick-effect styrene. Once this idea had seeded, it indicated the way forward.

Work commenced by pushing out the etched window-frames and removing the rear lean-to extension using a fine-toothed pull saw. This was put to one side and will, no doubt, reappear in some other role at a later date.

All external detail, with the exception of the window frames, was then shaved off with a heavy craft knife. The resin cuts and carves away readily enough and can be cleaned up with an emery stick. The most challenging part to remove was the name

Hornby's Skaledale village hall modelled in resin.

The rear extension, which had been cut off from the rear of the village hall.

The basic building shell with the windows removed and details cut and sanded off.

board above the front door because it was difficult to get a blade flat beneath it. It was ground off using a burr in a mini-drill. Brick-effect styrene sheet was then cut to cover the walls, with apertures cut out to match the positions of the window frames and door-ways. The side-walls were cut 50mm over-length at the rear, this excess being supported by panels of 60 thou styrene. These were the walls for the rear kitchen extension. Once prepared, these walls were glued to the Hornby shell with UHU glue and the rear extension, intended to be the kitchen, made up with more 60 thou and brick sheet. A flat, concrete-slab roof was fabricated for the rear extension.

The Wills corrugated asbestos was cut to size and the eaves' edge prepared by sanding it thin and then filing matching corrugations on the underside (the Wills packaging shows the method). Again UHU was used to fix the roofing in place. Capping stones from scribed styrene were fitted on the tops of the rear-extension walls.

With the basic shell complete, concrete styrene window-sills, lintels and barge boards were added, followed by guttering and downpipes. The guttering is styrene tube split along its length and the down-pipes are made from styrene rod carefully bent while cold in round-nosed pliers. The rear downpipes and hoppers serving the flat roof are made up from parts of the Wills guttering kit.

The ridge for the asbestos roof was formed from tube with pin-striping masking tape, 0.75mm wide, forming joints between individual sections. Punched discs finished off the ends. A brick chimney-stack, left over from the conversion of the Walthers office building kit, fitted on to the flat roof over the kitchen area. Lead flashing around the base of the chimney and at the rear of the flat roof was represented by strips of masking tape sprayed gunmetal grey.

Windows are the Hornby originals but, where required, new window-frames were made up from thin styrene strip.

A view from the rear showing the flat-roofed kitchen extension, the walls clad in brick-effect styrene and the roof covered with Wills corrugated asbestos.

The largely completed building with rainwater goods, windows and concrete sills and lintels fitted. A notice board hangs on the front wall.

From the rear the chimney serving the kitchens is seen along with the kitchen doors, light and windows.

The completed canteen sits on its temporary base. The signage decal was homemade and snuggled down with Solvaset to look like it had been painted directly onto the brickwork.

The rear service doors with smaller bins from the Peco Modelscene range and a larger bin made up from styrene tube and rod. Various works vehicles go about their business.

A noticeboard was fixed to the front wall, where it would see considerable passing traffic as workers visited the canteen. It is a simple styrene box with an acetate front and three small paper notices sit within it. After painting the details in house colours, the brickwork and roof were lightly weathered before the windows with their pre-painted glazing bars were replaced. As mentioned earlier, at a very large industrial site, there might be two or three canteens serving different departments.

Nobody wanted to spend half of their lunch hour walking to and from a distant building, so it will be conveniently situated for the melting shop. The model was lettered as 'Melting Shop Canteen' with home-printed decals. A number of smaller details can be seen in the photographs: lights, cabling, vents and pipework serving the kitchen at the rear. A couple of dustbins sit by the rear door.

CONCLUSION

The canteen currently shares a sub-baseboard with the works laboratory. When finally installed on the layout, the two buildings will be placed side by side with a roadway running between them. They will face the melting shop, and be separated from it, by a railway line and another roadway. The railway line will serve the slag lines running into the side of the melting shop building.

On reflection it would have been almost as easy to have built this canteen from scratch, but the project demonstrates an extensive rebuild of a resin building. These resin buildings offer all sorts of possibilities beyond their designer's original intentions. Also, despite the modifications, it has kept the interesting shape that attracted me in the first place.

CHAPTER TEN

ROLL SHOP

THE PROTOTYPE

No, this is not an extension of the catering facilities. The roll shop illustrated might be more fully referred to as a Roll Maintenance Shop and its function is the care and refurbishment of the rolls used in the rolling mill. This particular building was erected at the Irlam works in 1955 and housed machine tools, mainly lathes, used to turn the rolls as part of their maintenance schedule.

Rolls are cast from certain grades of iron and sometimes from steel, and they essentially comprise four sections. The central portion is the rolling surface with turned 'flanges' or cuts that control the shape of the material being rolled. Either side of this, are two flat, polished surfaces, which sit in the bearings in the mill housing. At one end of the roll there is either a flat or a cruciform end-piece cast as part of the roll. When the roll is installed on the mill, this end-piece sits in a heavy, cylindrical, 'wobbler box', which is a simple, yet robust, universal drive. This arrangement allows the roll to move up and down in the mill housing in relation to the incoming drive shaft from the mill motor.

Lancashire Steel's new roll maintenance shop under construction showing the office amenity block at the rear. TATA STEEL EUROPE

A side view of the building with the distinctive windows and roof lights visible. TATA STEEL EUROPE

A new roll being fitted into the 40in Lamberton cogging mill at Lancashire Steel's Irlam works. Note the absence of hard hats, which are mandatory today. **TATA STEEL EUROPE**

Rolls have an arduous life: white-hot steel is slammed into them, cooling water sprayed on them and they run miles and miles across the surface of the steel sections being rolled. Continuous casting has seen the demise of most heavy rolling mills. These are, or were, the largest rolling mills, the cogging or blooming mills, and were used to roll ingots down to blooms. Medium- to small-sized mills are still used to produce the finished steel product, which might be a section of some description, plate or sheet. Whatever the size of the roll, it will wear, the corners will round off and it will need to be 'dressed', i.e. have its profile re-cut. That is where the facilities in the roll shop come into play, either cutting new rolls to the required profile or extending the useful life of the rolls by re-cutting them. Eventually the roll will become too worn for further use and it will be scrapped and recycled back to the roll foundry.

The Irlam roll shop building itself is a fairly anonymous construction with three-quarter-height brick walls and upper walls and roof of corrugated asbestos. It features large metal-framed windows and clear corrugated roof lights providing good internal lighting. One end of the shop has a two-storey brick

The interior of the roll shop at Port Talbot Works – it's basically a machine shop. The rolls seen have flat sides as they are designed to roll flat sheet. **TATA STEEL EUROPE**

office and an amenities' block projecting from it. The unseen end has a large doorway allowing rail access for wagons carrying rolls to and from the mill and the inside of the building was served by an overhead crane of, perhaps, 25-ton capacity. A building of this

A building of not dissimilar design currently standing in Lydney, Glos. Brick walls with corrugated asbestos upper walls and roof.

sort could be built in any size, with or without the office extension, and with half-height, quarter-eight or dwarf brick walls. As a modelling exercise it presents an alternative to the corrugated iron 'big black shed', providing large-scale accommodation for any industry or activity of your choice.

THE PROJECT BUILD

The construction of this model used four main materials: foamboard, brick-embossed styrene sheet, Wills corrugated asbestos with their matching glazing sheet and steel-framed windows from my own etches. These window frames could be cut from a Scalelink fret, drawn direct on to the glazing material with paint and a bowpen, or made up from styrene strips. All of these methods have been used on one or other projects in this book. The sheet of window frames, which I had etched from my own artwork, included frames for the roll shop. Styrene sections and other bits naturally play a part in the small details. Printed brickpaper is an alternative to the embossed brickwork; both have their own advantages.

The building was not modelled full length. On the finished layout it will 'emerge' from the backscene at an angle a little to the right of the melting shop. I redesigned the plan of the original building to suit my own needs. Instead of having a full-width office at the rear, I moved it to the front, made it just half-width

and left space for a large door on the other half. This door allows rail and road access into the building.

CONSTRUCTION

Construction commenced by cutting out the walls and roof, including those of the front office, from 5mm foamboard. A sub-base was then cut from 10mm board. Apertures for windows and doorways were marked out on the wall sides and also cut out. The window apertures were cut to be oversized for their corresponding etched frames to allow space for the styrene window sides. I bought and printed off some Scalescene's white brickpaper. This was applied to the inner walls along the sides and rear.

It was planned that the large door would be left open with a view into the building's interior. Applying brickpaper to the inner walls hides the bare foamboard. The walls and roof were than assembled with PVA. Foamboard corner brackets and roof-profile formers kept the assembly square while the glue hardened.

As with any foamboard carcass that will later be clad with styrene, the corner joints were cut to be flush. With the construction complete, the walls were clad with sheets of pre-painted, brick-embossed styrene sheeting fixed with UHU. The cladding was not fitted right to the top of the side-walls, just a little higher than the point where the bottom edge of the asbestos cladding would later be fixed. Narrow

The basic 5mm foamboard shell. The upper walls have 10mm foamboard packing to bring the asbestos cladding out over the buttresses.

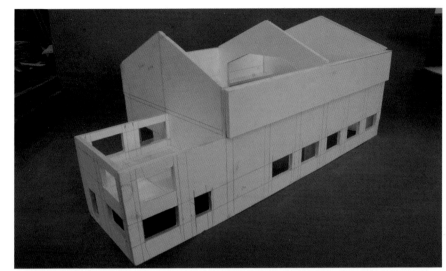

ABOVE: *A buttress under preparation.*

RIGHT: *Brick-embossed styrene sheet fitted, buttresses in place and corrugated asbestos fitted to the upper walls.*

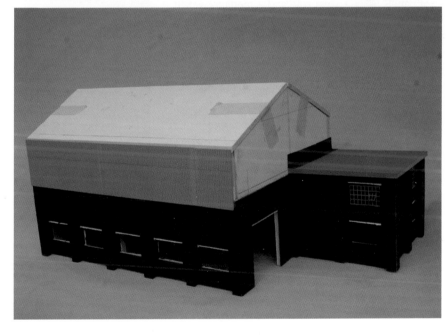

strips of the brick styrene sheet, about 5mm wide, were fixed with solvent into the sides of the window and door apertures, and similar strips of plain styrene fixed to the tops and bottoms. These give apparent depth to the walls and allow the window frames and doors to be inset from the wall surface.

The original building featured narrow, brick buttresses. These were made up from 20mm wide strips of 5mm foamboard, clad on the front and both sides with brick-embossed styrene sheet, and fixed to the walls with UHU. Solvent was run down the joint where the styrene sheet on each buttress met the styrene on the main walls.

Before applying the upper-wall cladding it was necessary to bring out the foamboard walls to match the depth of the buttresses. Panels of 5mm foamboard were applied to them. At this point the flat office roof was fitted made from 5mm foamboard, covered in 240 grit paper, and spayed with Suede effect paint.

ASBESTOS CLADDING

The upper walls were then clad with Wills corrugated asbestos sheets held on with UHU. These panels are easy to work with and invisible vertical joints are readily made by cleaning up the edges and pushing adjacent sheets together with plenty of solvent in the joint. The solvent softens the edge of the material and the sheets merge together. A little light sanding soon removes any excess plastic from the joint.

The roof was clad next, the sheets being prepared like a jigsaw and the roof light positions marked out with a pen.

I copied the Irlam prototype and incorporated three rows of staggered, clear, roof lights. These were 19mm squares cut laboriously out of the thick roof panels using a steel rule and a medium-weight craft knife. The clear panels were rather more easily cut from the matching, but much thinner, Wills clear corrugated sheeting. They are held in place with cyanoacrylate adhesive.

As suggested on the Wills packaging, the edges of the 'asbestos' sheet, where they overhang the roof edges, were thinned with a coarse sanding stick and shaped with a needle file, giving the effect of a thin, corrugated edge. This takes a little while but does greatly improve the appearance. On the prototype the corners of the walls, gable ends and the roof ridge are covered with pre-cast asbestos cement profiles. I used thin L-shaped styrene sections for the corners and made the ridge profile from two narrow strips of 10 thou styrene laid along its length. A piece of styrene tube, long enough to cover the ridge, had narrow strips of pre-cut masking tape wrapped around at 30mm intervals to suggest individual lengths of asbestos ridge fittings. This tube was glued along the ridge and small discs of styrene fitted at either end finished off the ridge detailing.

THE BASE

The real building sat on a large concrete slab. To replicate this, a length of code 75 track was fixed with PVA onto the 10mm foamboard sub-base. The 'slab' itself was planned to give a narrow plinth around the sides of the main building and to extend forwards at the front by 150mm to accommodate the office and

The office building with its roof fitted and some windows trial fitted.

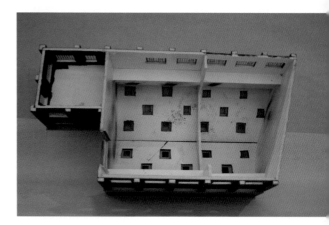

Inside the building's shell showing the foamboard structure.

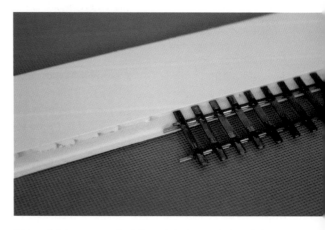

To make inset track, the edge of a piece of 5mm foamboard is rebated allowing it to clear the sleeper ends and butt up against the rail edge.

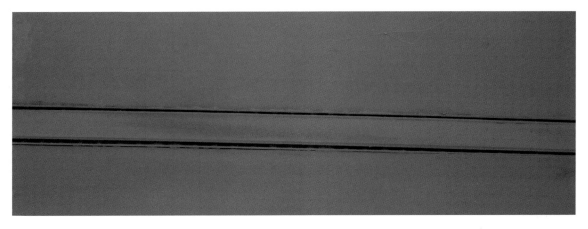

*The base, sprayed with suede-effect paint, showing the inset track. The infill
is a strip of styrene between the two inner guide rails.*

a small yard. This floor was built up on the sub-base, either side of the track, with 5mm foamboard and a little filler was used in any gaps between the foamboard edge and the rails.

The middle of the track had two inner check rails, made from code 75 rail, glued in place making sure that there was sufficient clearance for rolling stock wheels. Between the check rails the level was built up using layers of styrene sheet until a flush floor surface had been obtained. Once completed, the surface was sprayed with suede-effect paint and the top surfaces of the rails wiped clean with cotton buds.

The etched window-frames were prepared in the same manner as outlined in Chapter 4 and fixed into their apertures with Klear. Doors and doorframes for the office extension were made up from styrene.

DETAILS

A large, shutter door was installed over the main doorway. It comprises fabricated U-channel runners fitted into the door aperture and a 'box', to accommodate the rolled door and its mechanism, fitted across the top. The door itself, modelled largely open, is a piece of corrugated styrene sheet fixed into the runners and to the top 'box'. Some corrugated styrene has a series of rather flat and wide corrugations, and is well suited to representing the narrow, flat metal strips from which roller doors are made. As the open door gives a view into the building, I will, at some point, add some

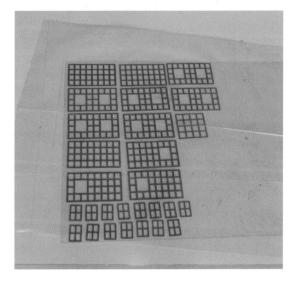

*The etched window-frames painted and glued
with spray adhesive to clear glazing material.
The clear polythene will be wrapped above and
below it and the whole weighed down overnight.*

representations of machine tools. These will not be very detailed as the building itself will be at the back of the steelworks' model.

Guttering will be modelled from styrene tubing cut in half to form channels, with drainpipes from narrower tube fixed to the walls with twists of wire.

The yard at the front features some roll-storage racks made up from styrene I- and H-section. Rolling mill rolls can weigh several tons, so these racks need to be substantial. The rolls themselves are either

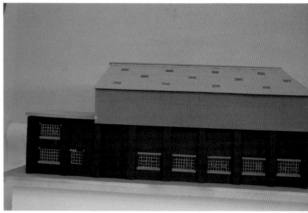

A completed window temporarily fitted into the building showing the opening sections.

A side view to compare with the prototype pictured earlier. Some of what is seen is temporary and the building requires properly bedding in.

from RT Models or are made up from lengths of styrene tube. The RT Models' rolls represent larger plate mill and cogging rolls. They are cast in resin and just need a little cleaning up. As supplied, they have a flat drive extension on one end. These are prototypical but I change them to a cruciform drive by the simple addition of two bits of square styrene strip. Smaller rolls can be made up with styrene tube representing the basic roll with narrow sections of wider tube forming the turned ridges.

Other bits lie around the yard, e.g. oil drums and old crates. Before World War II, a railway crane would have served the yard, loading and unloading the rolls, as required. By 1960 a road crane would have been just as likely to be called over; a Coles' yard crane from Oxford completes the scene.

In one photograph a still glowing roll, fresh from being cast in the foundry, sits cooling off on an internal user wagon. This scene was inspired by photographs of R. B. Tennent's roll-making foundry, which stood at Whifflet near Coatbridge until closure in 1995. Tennent's had a well-kept fleet of steam Sentinel locomotives and a number of enthusiasts paid them visits over the years. Some steelworks did cast their own rolls but most bought them in from the specialist founders.

The roller shutter doorway.

The works' Sentinel delivers a roll still hot from being cast in the foundry. Some temporary detail and clutter is seen along with a mobile crane awaiting its next task.

CONCLUSION

As can be seen, the roll shop was not quite finished when the photographs were submitted for publication. The windows and doorways are temporary, detail was minimal and a general tidy up was required. Hopefully, it still demonstrates the method of construction.

This was clearly a much more straightforward build than the open-hearth melting shop. However, the two share a common theme: that of the anonymous, sheet-clad, industrial building, which could, and did, house any number of activities. This building could have been clad in corrugated iron and the melting shop in corrugated asbestos. By combining the techniques and materials used and described in these two projects, many buildings can be modelled suitable for any heavy industry.

CHAPTER ELEVEN

COOLING TOWERS

THE PROTOTYPE

Many industries heat water as part of their processes. This may just be modest quantities of hot water used as part of a cleaning process, through to vast volumes turned to superheated steam for power generation. All of these plants need to cool this water after use and before it can be recycled or returned to a drain or natural water source. A variety of cooling systems, each suited to the volume of water to be cooled, are in use. Low volumes are cooled in small plants, some of which may be roof-mounted and are essentially a heat-exchanger, something like a very large car radiator, through which powerful fans draw cooling air.

By its nature, where heavy industry heats water, it is usually in large volumes and very often to high temperatures. Examples of such industries are power-generation stations, coke-oven plants, petrochemical plants and steelworks. As a consequence of the amounts of hot water generated, the cooling plant provided is large in scale and often a major feature of the industrial facility. Such cooling towers are often very tall, up to 200m (656ft), and so dominate not just the industrial facility itself, but the surrounding landscape too.

There are basically two types of large, industrial cooling tower: the forced-draught type and the natural-draught type.

FORCED-DRAUGHT COOLING TOWERS

Forced-draught cooling towers use powerful fans to drive cold air through a heat-exchange unit; again, something along the lines of an enormous car radiator. This type of cooling system is relatively compact, perhaps 20m (66ft) tall and 50m (164ft) long, though they can be bigger. They are usually rectangular blocks with sides open to the atmosphere via large, louvered or meshed sides to allow the ingress of cooling air. The water to be cooled is pumped inside into large heat-exchange matrices. Along the top, or sometimes along the sides, are a series of large, circular housings in which run large fans. These fans draw cooling air through the sides, over the heat-exchange matrices and up and out through the top of the unit. This constant flow of cool air, the forced draught, absorbs the heat from the hot water and takes it out into the atmosphere. Cooling towers of this type have become more popular over the years, though they do require energy input to drive the fans. A cooling tower of this type can be seen under construction in the first photograph in Chapter 13.

NATURAL-DRAUGHT COOLING TOWERS

It is the natural-draught type that is generally envisioned when the phrase 'cooling tower' is mentioned. These striking and often very tall structures dominate for miles around, which is why we are so familiar with them. In the natural-draught type, the water to be cooled is pumped partway up the heart of the structure. There it is sprayed on to a framework of internal wooden slats down which the water runs. These slats present a large surface area over which the water runs as it flows down. The heat in the water warms the air in the body of the cooling tower and the air starts to rise. As it rises, it draws in replacement cold air at the bottom. A cycle of cooling is initiated: the warm water descends and gives up its heat to the rising column of air being drawn in from below. The result is cold water collecting in a pond over which the tower stands, with warm air and water vapour issuing from the top. The typical concrete hyperboloid or 'pepper pot' cooling tower seen at power stations is of the natural-draught type.

Cooling towers standing at Ratcliffe-on-Soar power station in Nottinghamshire.

All share a basic form of a lower body tapering into a narrow waist and then flaring out towards the top. The proportions of these forms do vary. Some towers have more prominent waists and the waist's position can vary from a little over halfway up, to almost at the top, such that the top section is quite shallow. The Bechers' book on cooling towers features some other profiles of both concrete and wood in Continental Europe unlike any I have ever seen in the UK.

On many towers there is a marked block pattern visible on the sides, which results from the method of construction. Concrete cooling towers are built upwards by fabricating the support legs first. On top of the legs a circular formwork trough is constructed, which is divided into segments with formwork cross-walls. Concrete is poured into the segments one by one and the dividing formwork removed. Once a complete ring of these segments is complete, and the concrete set, the formwork is removed, moved up one level, and the process repeated. As the build progresses, the formwork is positioned to develop the required inward taper towards the waist, and then tapered outwards to the top. It is the joints between the successive segment and level casts that gives rise to the blockwork effect; they are not mortar lines. Bachmann have considerably overdone this effect on their Scenecraft offering, which, with its deep grooves, almost resembles a block of chocolate.

There is, or was, another type of natural-draught cooling tower in use at some industrial sites. Working on exactly the same principle as just outlined, these towers were constructed of externally braced, treated, wood. They were rectangular in plan with a raised centre section acting as the vent for the rising warm air. Such towers saw use at power stations, gas works and steelworks and, though lasting well into the later years of the twentieth century, it is probable that there are no longer any standing.

One of the Ratcliffe-on-Soar cooling towers – a typical natural-draught concrete tower.

THE PROJECT TOWER

Prototype concrete cooling towers can be truly enormous, up to 200m (660ft) tall and 100m (328ft) in diameter. Such a structure in 4mm scale would exceed a dustbin for size – not only impractical for many modellers, but its sheer bulk would overwhelm even a very large layout. Fortunately many are considerably smaller and, using the principles of proportion and compression, it is possible to model a realistic and imposing model to suit many layouts. One or two would make a spectacular centrepiece for a model of a power station.

THE CONSTRUCTION

The project tower is 550mm (22in) tall, 400mm (16in) in diameter at the base, and construction is started by sketching out, on graph paper, the proposed tower to full size. This gives a good feel for the size of the completed model, enables a good shape to be developed and provides a source of measurements for the four circular formers that are the starting point of the build.

It is worth pointing out that though a two-dimensional drawing will give some idea of the size of the final model, it will not give any indication of its sheer bulk.

THE SUB-STRUCTURE

Taking measurements from the drawing, four discs were cut from MDF, the disc for the 'waist' from 10mm board, the other three from 2mm board. These can be cut with a jigsaw, scroll saw or a router. The 2mm MDF discs could be cut with a circle cutter and the thicker 'waist' disc laminated from four of five thin discs. The project discs were cut out with a jigsaw, the results being more than acceptable, though they were then tidied up on a router table.

The centres of the MDF discs were then drilled 8mm and the discs, along with washers and nuts, were positioned along a length of 8mm-diameter threaded rod as shown in the accompanying photograph. The nuts are used to position and lock the discs into position so that they match the desired profile. At this stage only the top, bottom and 'waist' formers were fixed in their final positions, while the lower intermediate former was temporarily positioned at a lower position.

The next stage was to clad the formers with narrow strips of MDF cut long enough to allow for a 40mm rim above the top former and a 20mm rim below the bottom former. These strips of 2mm MDF, 20mm wide, were cut using a heavy craft knife and straight edge. Cutting relatively thick material such as

The four circular MDF formers.

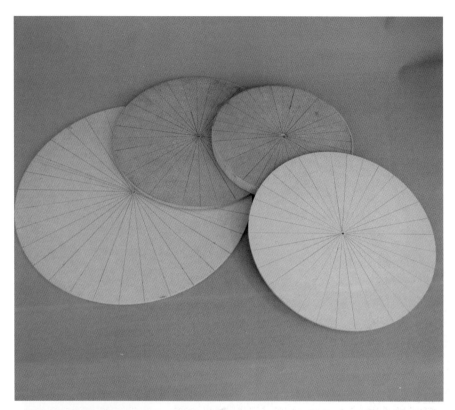

The formers threaded onto the studding and held in their relative positions with nuts.

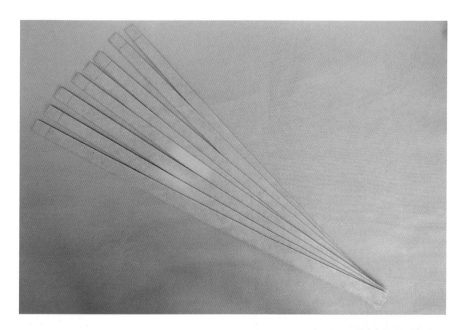

Strips of 2mm MDF, which will form the basic shell structure.

this with a craft knife requires care; several lighter cuts are a safer method than trying to cut too deeply with fewer cuts. Even so, it did not take long to prepare sufficient strips to completely clad the structure. Before cutting commenced, two horizontal pencil lines were drawn across the MDF board. These marked where they should lie against the 'waist' former and, after cutting, small holes were drilled between these lines along the centre of the strip.

The strips were then fixed, using PVA glue, one by one to the structure using the pre-drawn pencil lines to align them with the smaller, 'waist' former. Small screws were used to firmly hold the strips to this, the natural spring in the MDF holding it firm against the other formers. Working round the tower, the strips were positioned tight against each other at the waist, gaps forming between them as they flared out into the parabolic shape at the other formers. Before the final formers were fitted, and whilst there was still a large enough gap between them, the loose, intermediate former was gently moved into position, lightly against the MDF strips. It was done at this stage so that a natural curve developed between the waist and the base, rather than run the risk of this former distorting the shape. PVA was run into the joints between this former and the strips. Whilst the gap was there, the threaded rod was removed, the

Assembly underway with the strips fitted to the formers. The small screws holding them to the thicker waist former are visible.

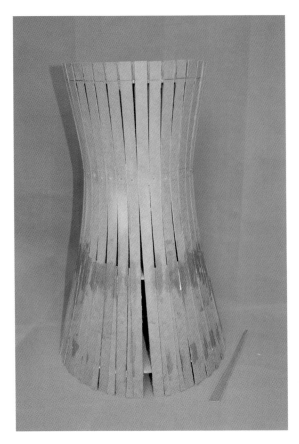

Cladding almost complete with infill pieces being added to the gaps between the strips at the bottom.

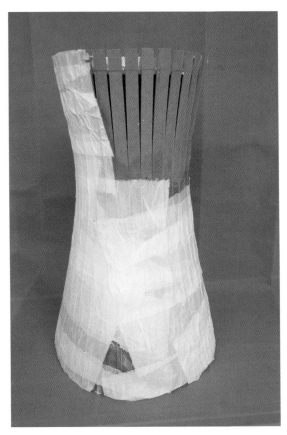

Heavy duty, PVA-soaked, kitchen-roll being applied in layers over the surface.

gap allowing access to the nuts. The final strips were then fitted and the whole left to dry.

Using a power-sander and a sanding block to work around the entire structure, a start was made in smoothing off the edges of the panels and starting to develop a round profile.

CLADDING THE SHELL

The body was then strengthened by wrapping PVA glue-soaked strips of kitchen-roll around it. This can take a little time and is a fairly mindless task, so layers were added over four or five days, the shell then being allowed to dry for several days.

Cooling-tower shells are supported at their base by a series of angled, reinforced-concrete legs, the gaps allowing the important cooling air to enter. These were cut from 4mm MDF using a template

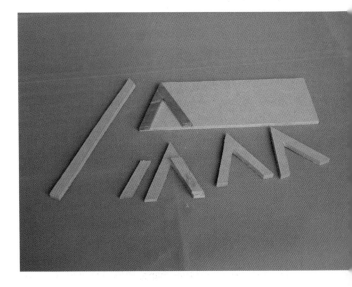

The legs being cut from 5mm MDF using a brass template and a heavy craft knife.

Clamps hold the leg assemblies in place while the PVA adhesive sets.

made from brass. The legs were bulked out with lower strips of MDF. This created a ledge on the leg that mated with the lower edge of the tower. The legs were held in place with PVA and strips of kitchen-roll binding them to the main body. This has proved to be a very secure method of attachment. To fit them full-depth around the base would require some accurate measuring and manufacture but, fortunately, as I was 'standing' them in water, the bottoms are not visible and so they did not need to meet.

The final outer layer was added by 'painting' on a thin mix of water-based interior filler. This can be bought ready-made and then watered down or mixed up from a powder; both were used on the model. The consistency was stiff yet brushable and over a period of several days, a number of layers were brushed on. After a few layers, the surface was gently sanded, between the application of layers, to start to develop the round shape. This creates a lot of fine

dust and is a job best-suited to an outside location. After several alternate sessions of sanding and filler, a good shape started to emerge.

At this point a happy coincidence involved the use of smooth masonry paint on a domestic outside project. This thick, easy-flowing paint seemed to offer promise as a final coating for the cooling tower, and so it proved. To aid quick and smooth paint application, I made up a simple wooden frame clamped into a workbench. The threaded rod was run back into the cooling tower and through the wooden frame, so the tower was mounted in a spit-like manner. A strip of wood and some nuts and studding formed a crank handle so that the entire cooling tower body could be slowly rotated whilst the paint was applied. Once dry, the masonry paint has an almost plastic nature and was cleanly cut to tidy up the corners of the legs. Several coats were applied, slowly building up a good external finish.

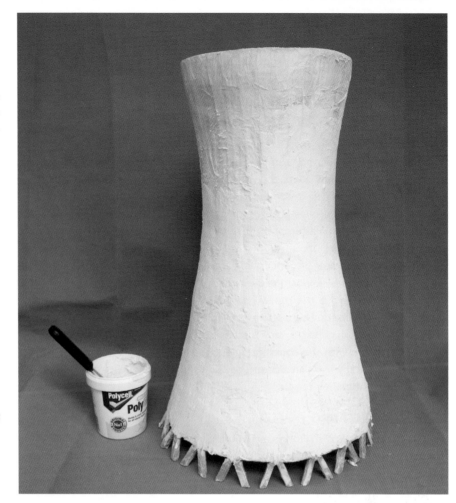

RIGHT: *Water-based DIY filler being applied over the surface of the tower.*

BELOW: *The tower mounted on its 'spit'. It has had several coats of tinted masonry paint applied whilst being turned. The styrene strip forming the top flange is shown being fitted.*

A top rim was formed from 60 thou square section superglued to the top edge of the tower. Spring clamps held the strip in place whilst the glue set and then a second layer was added using solvent. For the final few coats, the white masonry paint was coloured with a combination of paint dyes – sand, beige and olive green, plus a dash of blackboard paint – in an attempt to develop a concrete colour.

The top disc was left in place. It could probably be cut out but it provides support for the overall shape and, once on the layout, the top will be above the eyeline of most viewers. The disc was painted with blackboard paint, which has a very matt finish, and then the hard line with the concrete colour of the inner rim was lost by using an airbrush to feather in the colour transition.

THE COLLECTING POND

The prototypes sit in a shallow pond bounded by a concrete wall where the falling cooled water collects. In most designs this wall supports the legs of the tower so that the collecting pond is contained entirely within the tower's circumference. Some towers sit in the pond itself, which is a little larger in diameter than the tower, and this arrangement was chosen for the model. A circle of the diameter required for the pond was cut from a rectangle of 10mm foamboard. From a second 10mm board, using the trammel cutter, a ring was cut, the same internal diameter as the pond and with an outer radius 10mm wider. When cutting a ring, always remember to cut the outer radius first or you will lose your centre point! Glued on to the first piece, the ring forms the wall of the collecting pond. Strips of 250gsm card were glued to the outer and inner faces of the wall, the inner face being 20mm deep, to cover the exposed foam, and this then painted in a suitable concrete colour: primer followed by Tamiya Buff acrylic, in this case.

A sub-base was cut from 10mm foamboard and the upper surface of this was treated to represent the pond water.

This was achieved by spraying on several thin coats of Montana gloss 'Greenblack'. This gave a good impression of murky water. The sub-base was then glued to the underside of the layers featuring the pond walls. Finally, the painted surface was then given several thin coats of a DIY gloss varnish using a 25mm brush. The varnish was brushed in a circular pattern, the brush marks replicating ripples moving out from the centre.

The tower itself is heavy, so the base was now framed in strips of thin plywood with support strips glued underneath, another jigsaw piece for the final build.

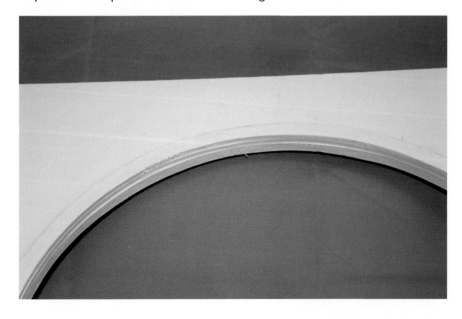

The base with a hole cut to form the pond and with a ring of foamboard fitted forming a raised wall around it.

The sub-base sprayed with Blackgreen paint and the base with pond cut out alongside.

ACCESS DOOR AND STAIRWAY

A Faller kit for a railway footbridge provided the parts for the stairway, which gives access to the door on the tower's side. This useful kit provides concrete steps and concrete landing towers, which can be useful in a number of applications. The kit steps were narrowed by cutting a strip off each side and then two flights were cut to size to provide the required overall height, i.e. to reach the position of the doorway. One of the smaller Faller towers provided the landing where the stairway turns through 90 degrees. These parts were assembled, cleaned up and painted with Tamiya Buff paint. Handrails from styrene strip completed the stairway.

Cooling-tower shells are generally devoid of much external detail – maybe an odd pipe running up the side. A few feature a latticework access stairway extending from ground-level up to the top rim. One feature most towers have, probably all, is a doorway located a little above the bottom. It provides access to the pipework and cooling sprays located in the base of the tower. The door is made from steel plate and generally elliptical in shape. This was a simple fabrication from styrene sheet, strip and with some thin rod forming the hinges. It sits in an appropriately shaped shallow depression cut and scraped out of the tower's shell.

Faller's footbridge kit – a useful source of concrete steps.

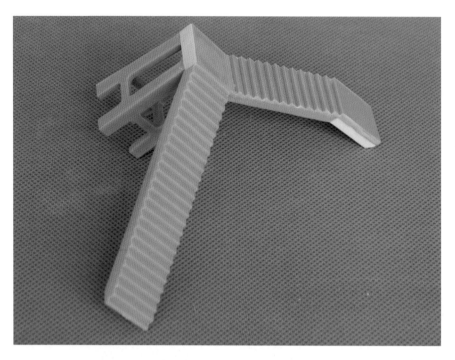

Access stairway made up and with white styrene used to fill any gaps.

FINAL DETAILS

The pumphouse, covered in Chapter 9, was positioned at the bottom of the tower. Some pipework will be added later from Plastruct components. As part of the company's safety policy, two lifebelts hang on a sheltered wooden stand, should anybody get into difficulties in the pond. The stand was a simple fabrication from styrene and the model lifebelts were obtained from eBay. They originally had over-scale rope loops moulded on, which were removed with a scalpel before the red banding was painted on.

A view showing the access stairway, the oval steel door in the cooling tower shell and a pair of lifebelts hanging in a rack.

A drone's eye view down towards the access stairway and the water filled pond.

The completed cooling tower.

CONCLUSION

I have yet to devise a satisfactory method of replicating the 'blockwork' effect prominent on many towers, though it is less apparent at a distance. I don't want to weather the tower until I have either developed a good method of modelling this block effect or have decided not to bother at all. Cooling towers weather in a very characteristic pattern – an ellipse of grime collecting on the lower section as it falls from the atmosphere with the prevailing wind. In the unlikely event of building another tower, the only modification I would make would be to reduce the size of the support legs. On the prototype they are often surprisingly slender. On the model, the application of many layers of paper towel and several coats of paint has made them quite chunky. It has, however, made a very strong structure – strong enough to sit on. I doubt there are many 4mm models that would survive that.

CHAPTER TWELVE

WATER TOWERS

THE PROTOTYPE

Water towers serve two purposes. First, they act as storage vessels or reservoirs ensuring that a supply of water is always on hand and, second, owing to their height, they provide a 'head' or pressure of water. The pressure is relative to the difference in height between the level of water in the tanks and the outlet point, wherever that might be, lower down. Many processes require water, and an interruption in supply might not just be inconvenient and costly but, where the water is used as a cooling medium, downright dangerous. Water towers are a feature of many industrial plants. Municipal water towers, those serving the public need, are sometimes ornately finished in brick and stone. Others, and especially water towers at industrial plants, are more functional, even brutal, in their stark simplicity.

STEEL WATER TANKS

Many steel tanks are made from relatively thin, square, pressed-steel panels, which have a strengthening pattern, often a star shape, formed in the centre, and with flanges to the edges. Two major suppliers of such tanks over the years were the South Durham Steel & Iron Company of Hartlepool and Braithwaite's of Newport in South Wales. The latter are still trading and an internet search will soon find their website.

The panels were riveted or bolted together, with a sealing strip, to form a tank of any required size or capacity. Water is not only very heavy but it also exerts considerable pressure on the tank sides. The insides of these tanks contain a network of diagonal struts holding the sides to the bottom and the sides to each other, though this bracing is not generally obvious when the tanks are full of water. The

The stark brutality of an industrial water tower serving the steelworks at Port Talbot. TATA STEEL EUROPE

thin steel base will be supported on several, closely spaced, heavy steel beams and a number of well-braced, vertical members hold the whole thing up in the air. Access ladders or stairways will be provided along with feed and outlet pipes and associated valves. Some tanks may have a top cover built as a shallow arc over the tank top.

Another type of steel tank, far more common in the United States, has a vertical, cylindrical body with

Alan Gibson etched fret for the Braithwaite design steel water-tank's panels and a section of the brass backing-sheet with bits of the 'L' and 'T' brass section soldered to it.

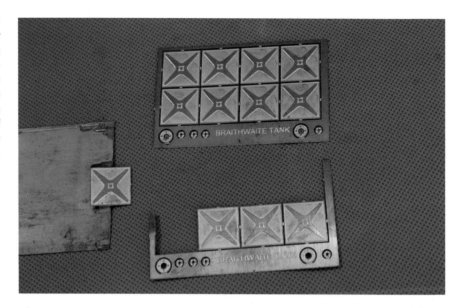

a hemispherical base and a flat or conical top. These stand on tall, tapering, steel lattice towers. They seem relatively rare in the UK, though one served the blast furnace plant at Shotton Steelworks and no doubt there were others. Models and kits of this type of water tower have been available from a number of US suppliers, Walthers being one.

STEEL WATER-TANK MODEL

The project tank was intended to sit alongside the open-hearth melting shop, which will be described in Chapter 14. One sat alongside the Shotton melting shop where I worked in 1974 and, exiting through the side-wall of the scrap stockyard and bound for the canteen, I would emerge at the same level as the tank base before descending on a metal stairway to ground-level.

THE TANK

The project model utilizes the sets of etched-brass water-tank panels available from Alan Gibson. Two patterns are available: one based on a Midland Railway design and one, as used here, based on a Braithwaite design. A pack contains sixteen square panels and, just as with the prototype, you form a tank of whatever size you require by combining any number of panels. Etched on to the fret are a number of useful pipework flanges.

The Gibson panels are nicely etched, though rather thin. The suggested method of assembly is to solder the panels to a framework of 1mm brass T- and L-sections. I wasn't entirely convinced that this would construct a tank with particularly flat sides or that it would it result in a robust enough final assembly, so I built the sides up on a sheet of thin brass. I assembled the components using solder and would not normally suggest anything other than this method where brass-to-brass joints are required. However, this is one assembly where superglue would probably work well enough. This model does not have to move and work, unlike a kit-built locomotive, and there are reasonable surface areas to take glue. I decided upon a tank three panels high with sides seven panels long and with ends four panels wide. That totalled sixty-six panels and so required five packs of the Gibson panels. Lengths of 1mm 'T' and 'L' and were obtained from Eileen's Emporium. Construction commenced by cutting out the brass panels from the Gibson fret. Most were kept in their original strips of four as they are correctly spaced for the final assembly on the fret. A length of the L-section brass was soldered along the long edge of the brass sheet and this would be the top flange of the tank. With this as a straight edge to work from, and using the strip of tank panels as a spacer, a length of T-section was then soldered, in parallel, along the brass sheet. Again, using tank panels

as spacers, a second length of T-section was soldered on, and finally a length of L-section. The latter forms the bottom edge of the tank. This whole process was repeated so that I had sufficient lengths of sections and backing sheet to form all four sides of the tank.

The brass backing sheet was cut along the edge of the inner L-section, resulting in tank sides of the correct height. By inserting the required number of panels as a measure, the sheet was cut into lengths to provide two sides and two ends. The Gibson panels were then soldered in rows between the brass sections. Short sections of flat, brass strip, sourced from scrap etch frets and soldered between the panels, formed the vertical ribs.

A base was cut from thick, brass sheet and the four sides were soldered to it, forming the tank. Small internal brackets ensured the corners were square. Lengths of L-section were soldered into each corner joint to complete the tank assembly. These finished the corners off very well. As the tank would have been full of water, no attempt was made to replicate the complex internal bracing, which would not be visible.

THE TANK-SUPPORT TOWER

With all four sides assembled, the tank was super-glued to a base of 60 thou styrene. This was cut larger than the tank base to allow for a walkway around the base.

Fifteen lengths of close-spaced Evergreen styrene I-section were glued to the base under the width of the tank, forming the top layer of the support framework. These sections were aligned under the tank joint lines and at their midpoints. The next layer of support comprised three deeper I-sections laid longitudinally. I had some Plastruct ABS I-section lengths that had been lying around unused for years. They are moulded with over-thick webs and flanges, and I rarely find much use for them. They do, however, have a decent depth and I thought they might be suitable here.

With the base of the tank well-supported, attention was then turned to the vertical support members. The height was set so that the base of the tank was level with the eaves of the melting shop scrap bay. The support framework comprises verticals and horizontals of H-section styrene with diagonals from round-section rod. These were made up as three identical flat frames, which were then assembled side by side with linking cross-members. The verticals were spaced so that they corresponded with the three main longitudinal girders beneath the tank. Quite a time-consuming task but it does result in a very sturdy-looking tank-support framework.

The main vertical members sit on small 'concrete' pads made from foamboard squares.

Rails were fitted around the walkway and a stairway constructed to link the walkway with the melting shop

The structural steel support tower made up from various styrene sections and rod.

Not quite complete – it awaits an access stairway and pipework – the steel water tower stands by the open-hearth melting ship.

and the ground. Access to the top of the tank was provided by a caged ladder. The final details were the addition of various items of pipework. An incoming feed-pipe runs from the ground and into the tank, an overflow pipe within the tank leads back to ground-level and an outlet leads from the bottom of the tank into the melting shop itself. All of the pipework and associated valves were fabricated from components found in a Knightwing/Walthers piping kit.

Painting was very quickly applied with a coat of primer, followed by spraying the support structure with two light coats of Humbrol Gunmetal from a spray can. The tank itself was airbrushed with my standard industrial green mix. The whole structure was finished by weathering using an airbrush. Details were highlighted by dry brushing and some further grime applied with weathering powders.

Finally, a water surface was provided from a piece of clear styrene sprayed on the underside with Montana 'Blackgreen' gloss. After fitting into the tank, two thin coats of Klear polish were brushed on to improve its water-like appearance. The 'water' looks suitably deep and dark.

CONCRETE WATER TOWERS

Reinforced-concrete water towers generally consist of a tank that is round in section, supported on various arrangements of concrete supports. The support might take the form of a massive, single, central column or be an arrangement of several legs arranged radially under the tank. A central column might be present, housing an internal stairway and various service pipes. These legs might be vertical or gently flare outwards from the tank base. Four or six legs are common arrangements, though very large tanks may have more. A tank of this type is a fairly easy scratchbuilding project using foamboard and readily available plumbing components.

CONCRETE WATER-TANK MODEL

The tank is simply a plastic-pipe reducer, 90–75mm, sold for use in Koi pond plumbing and was sourced on eBay for £3.25 (2016). The larger section was intended for the water tower and it has an external diameter of 105mm, an internal diameter of 90 mm, with a depth of 60mm. That scales up to a tank capable of holding around 6,000gal (27,240ltr) of water, which would weigh 22 tons (22,352kg). A section of suitably sized, plain, plastic pipe would be an alternative starting point.

I needed to cut all but 5mm off the smaller section. After marking the cutting line using a jubilee clip, I clamped the reducer in a large vice and removed the unwanted section with a fine-toothed handsaw. A clamping workbench would a good substitute for the large vice. Immediately its potential as a water tank becomes apparent: with its tapered transition between the main body and the base, it somehow looks just right.

The very shiny outer surfaces were sanded using a sheet-sander. This also removed some raised lettering that was moulded on to the rim and prepared the plastic to receive glue or paint by giving it a texture. This particular type of plastic was readily glued with Plastic Weld solvent and didn't require a PVC plumbing solvent.

A disc of thick styrene was cut and then glued to the bottom of the fitting. The tank sides were detailed with raised reinforcing rims and bracing. These were made from strips of 30 thou styrene glued onto the tank sides. Two layers were added to give some worthwhile relief. One layer of 60 thou would have been a possibility but would not have followed the curve of the tank body quite so readily. A little filler around the top gave a nice, flat and square, edge and rim.

The Koi pond plumbing fitting, which showed promise as the tank of a concrete water tower.

Cut into two, the section on the right starts to reveal its potential as a water tank.

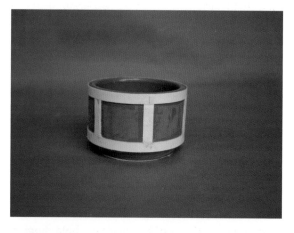

Styrene detail added to provide some relief and interest to the plain tank sides.

THE SUPPORT STRUCTURE

The legs and braces were cut from 10mm foamboard and care was taken to ensure the edges were cut square. The legs taper in width from 10 to 20mm, giving finished units 10 x 10mm at the top and 20 x 10mm at the bottom. The exposed foam faces are clad in 250gsm card using PVA adhesive. Six identical beams were made up in this manner.

Using a circle cutter, two discs were cut from foamboard, one 90mm in diameter from 5mm board for the top platform and one 150mm in diameter from 10mm board for the base. Both discs were very carefully marked out into six segments using a clear plastic protractor, each line marking the centre line for a leg. Using these centre lines, cutting guidelines, 10mm apart, were drawn onto the discs. The edges of both discs were then notched, 10 x 10mm on the top board and 20 x 10mm on the base, to provide accurate location points for the legs.

The six legs, the base and the top discs were then assembled and fixed with PVA. This assembly was checked for accurate alignment, held in shape with masking tape and then left to dry overnight. The notches cut in the top and base make accurate assembly a straightforward process.

I planned to provide the tower legs with two levels of support rings spaced 130mm apart. With the levels marked out on the legs, the distance between the outer faces of adjacent legs was measured. There are six legs with 60-degree angles between them so, as the beams have two ends, each end needs to be cut across at 30 degrees. In fact the end joints have a compound taper as the legs are not only at an angle to each other, but also flare out as they descend. This latter angle is small and was ignored in the cutting; a little filler will tidy everything up later in the process. If the legs have been assembled accurately, each cross-beam at the same level should be the same length. If not, each beam will have to be cut accordingly. With the assembly upside down the cross-beams were inserted in order, the taper of the legs held them at the right level, and PVA fixed them in place. A little fine-tuning is required to get them in line and bits of masking tape hold them in accurate alignment whilst the glue hardens. With legs,

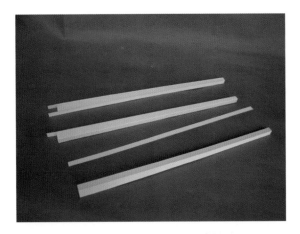

Making up the main support legs from tapered foamboard strips.

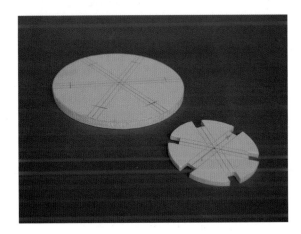

The top and bottom discs showing one marked out and one cut out, to receive and locate the legs.

A trial assembly showing how the legs fit into the notches in the circular discs.

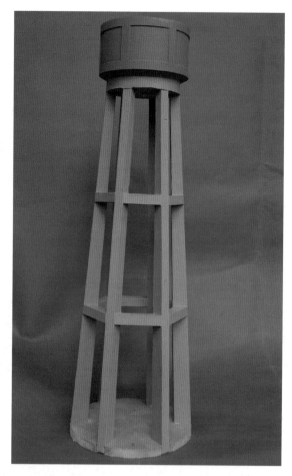

The basic assembly complete with horizontal supports fitted and the tower with a coat of tinted masonry paint. The plastic tank primed and sprayed with suede-effect paint.

top and base, and cross-beams assembled, the whole structure was examined, filler applied into any open joints and any other cleaning-up attended to. This assembly was then primed and given several coats of the masonry paint concrete-base mix. Checking and sanding between coats achieves a good uniform surface finish. Tank and base were sprayed with Plastikote Suede paint and then mated together. The exposed foam edges on both top and bottom discs were next clad with strips of 250gsm card and a further coat of Suede paint sprayed on.

Three inlet/outlet pipes, in this case made up and detailed from a Knightwing piping kit, were made up and run from the base of the tank vertically down the centre line to ground-level. A short length of plumbing pipe forms a sump under the base of the tank and the service pipes run down from this. At ground-level they disappear into a brick 'well', giving access to an underground service tunnel.

The only details on the tower are an access platform and caged ladders, the arrangement of which can be seen in the photographs. Essentially, a caged ladder runs up one leg to a service platform running under the tank. This provides access valves and extends outwards on the far side to serve a final ladder leading up to the tank top. The cage extends upwards above the tank rim and a short platform gives access to the tank interior.

For this model, etched-brass caged ladders from US supplier Gold Medal Models were used.

The pipework and valves being made up. White is styrene tube or sheet and grey is from Knightwing piping kits.

They require forming and soldering up and, being just 10-thou thick, need careful handling. Mounting 'staples' were bent up from thin, brass wire and soldered to the rear of the ladders. The foamboard legs were very easily drilled so that these staples could be inserted and held with UHU. The access platform and handrails were made up from styrene.

A paper template was used to plan out the access platform as it had to run under the tower, linking two ladders, and provide a walkway around the pipework running down the centre line. The brass fittings were primed and painted dark grey prior to being fitted to the tower. This was a rare use of soldering in the projects detailed in this volume; using caged ladders from Plastruct or Walthers would avoid the need for soldering. The Gold Medal ladder system makes up into a very fine caged ladder, though it is delicate and requires careful handling. It is also quite costly, since a single kit makes up just 175mm of ladder and a large industrial plant or complex might require several kits. The water tower needed three. It is not so readily available in the UK and though it worked well for this project, it hasn't been used elsewhere. Fitting the platform and pipework under the tower amongst the legs was a fiddly task and the final bits of handrail cannot be fitted until the ladders and access platform are actually in place.

FINISHING DETAILS

The tower was weathered using an airbrush and some weathering powders, working the grime onto the horizontal levels and corners where it would collect. Some rust streaks stain the concrete surface at the points where metal fixtures are attached and where stained water would have flowed down. The ladder and access platform were lightly dusted with rust- and soot-coloured weathering powders, and the handrails and ladder sides then wiped clean where hands and feet would have passed.

The water surface was replicated in a similar manner to that in the steel tank. A disc of clear acetate was cut to be a tight fit in the tank top and sprayed on the underside with Montana Greenblack paint. Clearly, when cutting a disc for such a use, it is not desirable to pierce the centre with the cutter

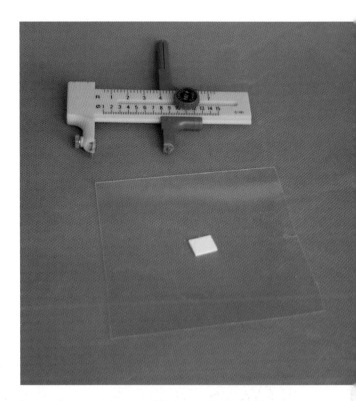

Preparing to cut out a disc from clear sheet to form the water surface. The white styrene square prevents the cutters pivot from piercing the clear sheet.

The clear disc, sprayed on the rear with Montana Blackgreen paint and punched for the overflow pipe which sits at the rear.

pivot. A small piece of 40 thou styrene placed on top of the clear material, and held in place with double-sided tape, provided the pivot point.

The disc rests inside the tank on a foamboard block, cut so that the acetate sits about 6mm inset from the top. Though the top surface of the acetate is already shiny, its water-like appearance was improved with a few thin coats of Klear floor polish. On the layout, by cutting a disc out of the baseboard top surface, the circular base of the water tower can be positioned into it and blended in with the surface finish.

The tower was temporarily placed near the works' canteen, where it demonstrated a striking contrast between the very human scale of the canteen and the size and brutality of this utilitarian industrial structure.

A drone's eye view of the completed tank.

A close-up showing the service platform and valves under the tank body.

Looking up at the completed and weathered tank.

CONCLUSION

The two tanks are very different models, produced by very different methods. They were both enjoyable to build and either is very suitable for a large range of industrial users. The steel tank, relying on commercial components, was obviously the most costly but the Gibson panels really do make the model what it is. Steel tanks of this type were also used by some of the railway companies and so have a wide range of applications for the modeller. Occasionally steel-panelled tanks have the company's name or something painted on them, a small detail that might be appropriate on some models. The very tall steel water tank at Dalzell Steelworks in Motherwell has long had the name 'Dalzell' painted on it. A Google search will find some photographs of it – I believe that it is still standing.

The concrete tower, apart from the optional etched ladders, cost very little to build yet it has resulted in an impressive structure that would grace many an industrial scene. The Koi Carp pond plumbing fitting was a fortuitous find and helped create a very plausible tank.

CHAPTER THIRTEEN

COAL-BLENDING PLANT

PROTOTYPE

Coke ovens turn coal into coke by heating it to incandescence in air-tight chambers or ovens. This drives off the volatiles as a hot vapour, which is collected and cooled, producing gas and a range of valuable chemicals. The coal does not burn in the oven as there is no oxygen to support combustion. The hot coke, virtually pure carbon, is pushed out, quickly cooled and used as a smokeless fuel or as a fuel and reducing agent in the blast furnace. Not all coals are suitable for coking – the end-user will demand coke of a particular specification, e.g. blast-furnace coke will not readily burn on a domestic grate. Consequently, great care is taken in the choice of coal and usually a specific blend of different coals is used.

There are a number of different methods of blending coal and the project model is of a type once used at a number of steelworks' and merchant coke-oven plants, e.g. East Moors at Cardiff, Clyde Ironworks near Glasgow and Irlam Steelworks near Manchester. Some plants had round silos, while others had square ones. In the photograph of the Irlam plant, it can be seen that the entire building is a rectangular block. Other square silo plants had them arranged corner to corner, giving the plant a saw-toothed profile. The plant consists of a series of vertical concrete silos, which are fed with coal from the top by a system of conveyor belts and trippers (gates that divert the coal off the belt and into a chosen silo). Different silos are reserved for different coals, perhaps four silos contain a Durham coal, another four a Yorkshire

A coal-blending plant under construction at GKN's East Moors Steelworks, which once stood at Cardiff Docks. In the foreground a forced-draught cooling tower is also under construction (see Chapter 11).
TATA STEEL EUROPE

An older design of blending bunker at Lancashire Steel's Irlam works. This had six individual silos and a total capacity of 2,000 tons of coal. TATA STEEL EUROPE

coal and a further two a Lancashire coal. At the base of the silos, gates control the volumes of the various coals being released on to the lower conveyor belt. By this method a controlled blend of coal is delivered on to the conveyor belt, which is then taken by other conveyors to the coke-oven service bunker.

Other blending methods involve the use of conveyors and travelling booms to build long heaps of coal along the ground. Each heap consists of layers of different coal types. These heaps are then drawn off in crosswise slices, producing a mix of coal of the required blend.

THE MODEL

Though this is a rather specialized structure, it is very like a block of grain or feed silos, so the techniques used in this build would be equally applicable.

One starting point for this build could be the Walthers ADM grain silo kit, though for the project, a larger model was to be built from scratch.

This model is a fairly straightforward project, as it is a plain structure with no complex shapes and little external detail. It is, however, large and, owing to the thick walls of the plastic pipe used, surprisingly heavy.

Concrete grain silos currently standing on the north bank of the Manchester Ship Canal between Eccles and Weaste.

The structure has four main components: a low block house-like base containing the blending gates and lower conveyor, the cylindrical storage silos, a housing running along the top of the silos covering the feed conveyor and a tall, rectangular structure at one end containing an access lift, stairways and services. All of these components are basically rectangular or cylindrical forms and can be readily constructed from foamboard and plastic plumbing pipe, as appropriate. A conveyor belt bringing in the crushed and cleaned coal leads up to the top of the structure and a second conveyor climbs away from the base, taking the blended coal away and on to the coke-oven service bunker.

CONSTRUCTION

THE SILOS

The first stage is to construct the silo assembly. Ten 290mm lengths of 75mm-diameter plastic plumbing pipe were cut, ensuring good square ends, and these were assembled in two rows of five. 75mm pipe was chosen simply because it looked right – better than the 65mm pipe I had in stock. It is not the most com-

monly available size and seems largely to be used in Koi Carp pond installations. I managed to find some in stock at a local Koi Carp dealer. It can also be sourced though suppliers on the internet. As this type of plastic does not glue that well, it was decided to hold the silo pipes together using small nuts and bolts. Whatever is handy will do – I used 4mm bolts. This necessitates drilling the lengths of pipe at top and bottom, so that the pipes can be bolted five in line and the two lines bolted together. To ensure the relevant holes were correctly positioned, a simple drilling jig was made up from offcuts of timber.

The holes were drilled 6mm, oversize for the bolts to be used, so there was some flexibility in final assembly allowing everything to be square and in line. Once I was satisfied with the assembly, thick beads of plumbing solvent were run into the valleys between each pipe.

This is quite a heavy structure so when the solvent was dry, a bead of frame sealant was run down each joint from a mastic gun for added strength. I did wonder initially whether or not bolting the pipes to each other was strictly necessary to ensure accurate assembly. However, on completion, the silo assembly is so heavy that I would be very dubious about

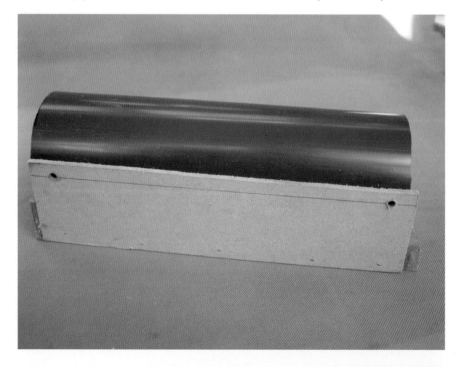

The MDF jig used for drilling the bolt holes in the silos.

The plastic tubes that form the silo assembly bolted together and glued. The thickness of the tube walls is apparent which gives the assembly its weight.

relying just on the solvent to hold it all together and so the bolts have remained in place. The valleys formed between adjacent pipes were then bridged with 25mm strips of 40 thou styrene acting as infills, and these were secured with liberal use of solvent. Care was taken to ensure that they were kept in line and in the same plane. I did consider making a jig to ensure accurate alignment. However, as there were only four per side, a dry run soon showed that simply holding a ruler across their ends kept them in line.

THE BASE AND TOWER

The next stage was to construct the base building and the tall, end tower. It was decided to build them as a combined L-shaped structure. The silo assembly set the width and length of the base building, 180 x 445mm, and the width and height, 180 x 290mm, of the end tower. A further 65mm was added to the tower's height to accommodate the top building. The other dimensions were determined by playing around with scrap bits of foamboard and drawings until suitable proportions had been realized. The base building is 65mm tall and the end tower 80mm deep. With the dimensions set, a start was made in cutting out side and end panels. It is always important to remember

to take into account the thickness of the materials being used in construction when marking and cutting out. This is especially important when working with materials 10mm thick. For example, though the buildings are 180mm wide, the inner cross-walls are only 160mm wide since there will be a 10mm outer wall on either side. Similarly, the side-walls were cut 10mm under height so that when a roof is added, the overall height is correct. Oversized window apertures were cut out along the sides and on the end tower; the correct-sized apertures will be cut into the styrene cladding.

Owing to the weight of the tubes above, inner cross-walls of foamboard were also cut and fitted to give some additional strength. Assembly started by gluing the large L-shaped sides to the base, then adding the tall end-wall and the cross-walls in the base. Masking tape held the structure together while the PVA dried. At this point the inner surfaces were sprayed matt black to help mask or hide the inner surfaces on completion. Considering the volume of coal that one of these plants would have processed over the years, no doubt the interiors would have generally been black in reality. The window reveals were also sprayed matt black. This is where the Foamex

10mm foamboard cut into a 'kit' of parts for the base and end buildings.

foamboard offers an advantage over the expanded polystyrene type. Automotive aerosols will dissolve the latter, whereas the Foamex remains stable.

With the PVA on the first assembly dry, construction continued with the addition of the tower's inner wall and the roof of the base building. The roof was cut to extend into the tower for added strength and the section outside the tower was cut an extra 5mm wide on either side. This was so that the edge would line up with some external strengthening ribs to be added later. The foamboard building shells were next clad in styrene sheet and all faces were covered, with the exception of the base.

Good-quality, double-sided tape was used to attach the styrene to the foamboard and the corners were bonded with solvent. For extra strength, 60 thou sheet was used for the roof of the base building, but 40 thou was used for all of the walls. Window

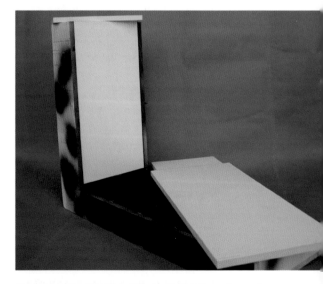

Panda eyes. Construction of the foamboard components underway with inner walls and window reveals sprayed matt black.

Three of the 40 thou styrene facing panels: the rear, one side of the tower and one of the base walls.

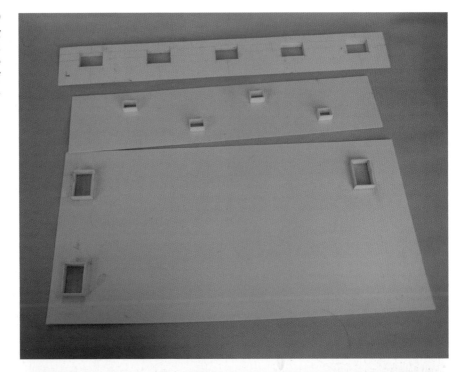

Fitting the styrene cladding with double-sided tape.

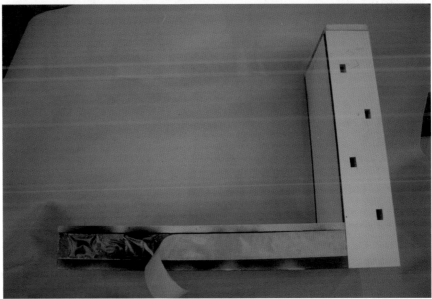

apertures were cut out of the styrene walls to accurately match the size of the Scalelink etched brass window sections.

These apertures were cut to be a close fit with the Scalelink windows, not too tight, just big enough to allow them to slip in. A window reveal was prepared from Evergreen strip and Slater's 40 thou square section.

The purpose of the reveals was for the flat strip to provide some depth to the walls and for the thin section to provide a constant depth backstop for the window frames.

The silo block with its top fitted, sanded to shape and with a rim around the top of each silo.

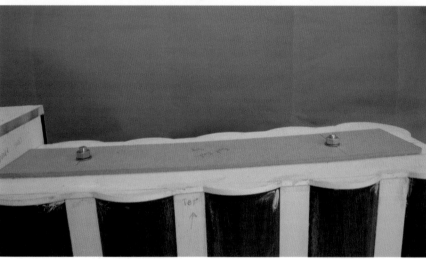

The top of the silo block showing the MDF strip and the tops of the studding and nuts that clamp the whole assembly firmly together.

The flat roof for the tops of the silos was also cut from 60 thou. The silos themselves were used to mark out the shape, which was cut and sanded to be an accurate fit.

At this point I developed a concern about the difference in weight between the heavy silo assembly and the lightweight foamboard construction of the base and side tower. Standing together there is no problem, but this structure would be moved around during the later parts of the construction and before its final positioning on the layout. I had a vision that if the building was ever tilted over, the silo assembly could just rip itself free, owing to its weight. Consequently, I decided to clamp the silo assembly

to the base structure using lengths of 8mm threaded studding. To facilitate this, a length of 5mm MDF was glued to the top of the silos and two smaller panels were glued on the underside of the base roof. This involved removing panels from the foamboard base to gain access. Had I thought of this first, the MDF would have been more thoroughly integrated with the base assembly.

Holes were drilled through the top and bottom to accept the studding. The silos were attached to the base using 5-min epoxy resin and the studding inserted though the holes. Nuts and washers were then fitted, run up moderately tightly, and the silos and base effectively clamped together.

THE TOP HOUSING

The top conveyor housing is a similar structure to the base building and was built in the same manner as a freestanding unit. It is 65mm tall and 445 mm long, but only 120mm wide as it does not extend to the full width of the silos. An upper extension was added where the conveyor bringing in the coal terminates. On the prototype, this top building contains a transfer station between the incoming conveyor and the top conveyor belt, and also contains the top conveyor itself and associated trippers, with maintenance access on either side.

All joints and corners were cleaned up with emery paper before scrubbing all external surfaces with Cif and then rinsing. Once dry, a coat of grey primer was applied, which helped to reveal any blemishes or gaps, which were attended to as required. The whole structure was then given a second coat of primer.

Next, two coats of suede spray paint were applied to suggest the rough cast of concrete. This building could not be any easier to paint – other than doors and window frames, it is all the same colour.

Windows are the almost obligatory steel-framed industrial style, in this case replicated using commercially available frets. Frames could have been made up from thin styrene strip or drawn on to clear sheet with a bowpen. Each window had been planned in advance with the frames cut from the Scalelink fret. This fret has frames of two sizes and I used the smaller set. The windows in the base building are ten panes wide by four panes tall, while those on the top conveyor housing are six panes by three panes. Smaller configurations were used on the sides of the vertical tower. As mentioned earlier in this chapter, window apertures had been cut in the styrene cladding to accommodate the brass frames. The frames

Assembly largely complete. The tube apart, all visible surfaces have been clad in 40 thou styrene.
Also visible are the external strengthening piers each made from two strips of 40 thou styrene.

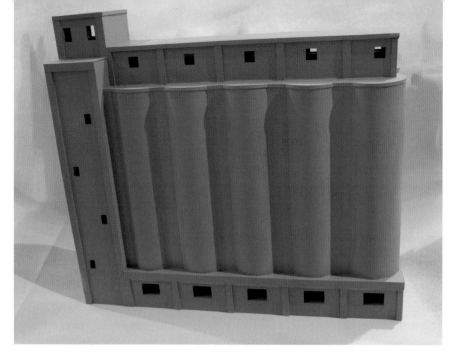

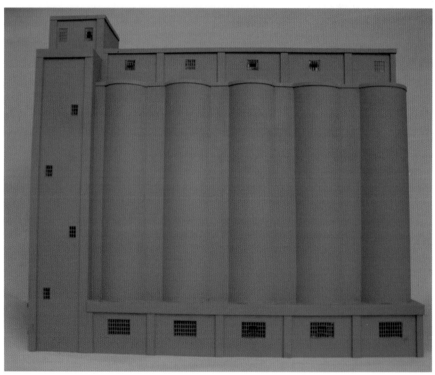

and glazing were prepared as outlined in Chapter 3. These windows usually have a hinged opening section and often these are left in the open position. On some of the windows, a section was cut out of the main frame and a small opening section cut from the Scalelink fret.

The windows were mounted into their apertures and held with Klear floor polish. The individual panes were also given a coat of Klear, which further bonds frame and glazing together.

Doors were made up from a combination of plain strip and Evergreen Novelty Siding. This is styrene sheet scribed at 3.8mm spacing and nicely replicates planking. The ground-floor doors are large, sliding doors and the rail on which the doors slide are just lengths of suitable Evergreen strip.

The completed coal-blending plant with windows, doors and smaller details fitted.

CONCLUSION

The coal-blending plant requires a few final details to be added prior to its installation on the layout. The structure will be served by two conveyors: one delivering coal from a ground-level wagon tippler up to the top conveyor housing, and a second taking the blended coal from the bottom conveyor on to the coke-oven service bunker. Conveyor construction has already been covered and the conveyors needed for this model will have foamboard cores, clad in Wills corrugated asbestos sheeting, as described in Chapter 5. It will also require some heavy weathering. A typical plant of this sort might handle a million tons of coal per year and that creates a lot of dirt and dust, so there's plenty of scope for adding grime.

This is the type of large industrial plant that depended entirely on the railways to function. As a model it is both imposing and unusual. It would provide a reason for running endless coal traffic. With little modification, a large grain-storage silo could have been built, which in turn would require trainloads of grain hoppers to service it.

When finally installed on the steelworks' layout, the blending plant will be adjacent to the coal tippler serving it. A conveyor will run from this tippler to a coal-crushing and grading plant, which is still to be built, with a second conveyor leading to the coal-blending plant. On a prototype plant there would be provision to take coal from the tippler to adjacent storage grounds by conveyor. When required, it could return either by conveyor or by internal-user rail wagons, which would take it to the tippler. This arrangement will be featured on the final installation.

CHAPTER FOURTEEN

OPEN-HEARTH MELTING SHOP

INTRODUCTION

The big black 'shed', a steel-framed structure clad, typically, in corrugated iron sheet, is certainly one of the signature structures of heavy industry. These buildings house a whole range of industrial activities and for the modeller they offer a number of opportunities. They can fill a corner even if only a gable end is modelled, gable ends or part relief sides can provide a dramatic backdrop requiring no more than an inch or so of space and they can very much set the modelling scene as industrial. With more space available, rail lines can be run into the buildings from the end, either along one side or along the central aisle, or transversely anywhere along the buildings' length. Buildings such as these are almost universally equipped with overhead cranes spanning their full width, so that railway wagons could be loaded/ unloaded anywhere within. Such a building on a layout provides a source of traffic and a reason to use some of the more specialized wagons available from the trade. As these buildings can be both anonymous and universal, it would be perfectly feasible to change the nature of the industry represented by simply swapping names, signs and maybe a few details. This week's 'Josiah Isherwood & Partners, Printing Machinery Manufacturers' could become 'The Dudley Chain & Anchor Works, est. 1843' next week.

Some of these buildings are relatively plain rectangular boxes devoid of much external detail other than doorways, whist others have quite complex shapes, such as multiple bays, extensions, ductwork, chimneys, walkways and windows. The project build is at the complex end of this spectrum, in fact probably as complex as these structures get. Any feature or construction technique required for this type of build is probably covered here.

A BRIEF HISTORY OF BULK STEELMAKING

Steel is a manmade alloy of iron and carbon along with small amounts of other elements and by selecting these other elements, and varying their amounts, thousands of steel specifications are available. These trace elements add specific properties to the steel, e.g. manganese gives hardness and durability, chromium confers corrosion resistance and vanadium gives increased durability at higher temperatures.

Steel has been known and has been in use for millennia. However, until the mid-nineteenth century, it was produced by very labour-intensive methods and in small quantities, making it a very expensive metal. It was reserved for weapons and tools, where its resilience and ability to 'take an edge' was invaluable. The structural metal, used for girders, joists and plate, of the early industrial years was wrought iron, a trade in which Great Britain dominated the world. A very useful material, wrought iron was considerably cheaper than the steel then available but it was nonetheless also produced by a very labour-intensive process. This changed in 1856 when Henry Bessemer announced his bulk steelmaking process, malleable iron as he called it, before the British Association for the Advancement of Science in Cheltenham. Though not without some serious initial flaws, it became, within a few years, a viable process for the rapid and cheap production of steel in bulk. Rather than being produced slowly in batches of a few tens of kilos, steel could now be made very quickly in convertors of, initially, 5-ton capacity and, later, very much larger.

It soon had a competitor in the open-hearth steelmaking process. In the late 1850s, Carl Wilhelm Siemens, a German who had taken British nationality and the first names Charles William, developed a regenerative furnace that used its waste heat to

Once installed on the layout, the bunkers will receive some heavy weathering and it will be served by a tippler and two conveyor belts.

preheat the incoming fuel and air. Not only was this very efficient, but it also enabled very high temperatures to be developed, temperatures suitable for steelmaking. In 1865, Frenchman Pierre-Emile Martin took out a user licence from Siemens and developed the open-hearth steelmaking process, sometimes referred to as the Siemens–Martin process. Though compared to the Bessemer method it was a slow process; a heat (the making of a single batch of steel) would take in the region of 14 hours, this made it very controllable and well-suited to the manufacture of a very wide range of high-quality steels. It was also versatile as it could be charged with hot metal (liquid iron), cold pig iron or cold steel scrap, either singly or in any combination. The steel could be sampled as the melt continued, and changes and additions made to bring the metal to the required standard within very close tolerances. Consequently, though the Bessemer process remained in use for a few particular applications, the open-hearth process soon overshadowed its competitor.

Between its inception in 1865 and the closing of the UKs last open-hearth melting shop at Shotton Steelworks on Deeside, at the end of December 1979, the process had accounted for something like 80 per cent of all steel produced in this country.

By the 1950s, with the cost of electric power falling, the already established electric arc process was becoming viable as a bulk steelmaking process and became increasingly widely used to recycle steel scrap. Also in the 1950s, the availability of oxygen in bulk saw the development of a range of new steelmaking processes, the LD process, the Kaldo process, the rotor process and spray steelmaking. Of these it was the LD process, now better known as the basic oxygen process, which became the bulk steelmaking method of choice where blast-furnace iron was available.

THE OPEN-HEARTH MELTING SHOP

As with most things industrial, in an open-hearth melting shop, form follows function. A brief explanation of both the plant and its operations will enable an understanding of why the building is arranged as it is and why railway lines enter where they do.

Open-hearth furnaces were housed in large, steel-framed, sheet-clad buildings that were rail-served from both ends. They are typically very long and are characterized by a line of tall chimneys, one per furnace, running along one side and, depending on their internal layout, may consist of a wide single bay or two or three parallel, adjacent bays. The furnaces were arranged along the buildings' centre line, standing on the edge of a massively constructed mezzanine floor.

The drawing shows a cross-section of a typical melting shop. The large, central bay is the melting shop itself with a furnace shown on the edge of the heavy mezzanine floor. The mezzanine floor is the charging floor from which raw materials are fed into the furnace and on the other side of the furnaces is the casting bay. Sometimes referred to as the pitside, the furnace is tapped into teeming ladles in this bay. High-capacity cranes, often able to lift 200 or 300 tons, carry these ladles over to the teeming stand where the ingot moulds, standing on heavy rail cars, are filled with the molten steel. Teeming is the term given to the process of filling the ingot moulds.

To the left stands the bay covering the raw material stockyard. This building will always be immediately adjacent to the melting shop. As drawn, the mezzanine floor of the charging bay extends across into the stockyard and the rail vehicles carrying the raw materials are delivered on to it via a long, inclined gantry. The raw materials are collected by the charging machines and dumped into the furnaces through the front doors. Another arrangement has the stockyard at ground-level and internal cranes lift the raw materials in charging pans up to the charging floor level.

The bay on the right is the ingot-stripping and mould-preparation bay. Here, once the ingots had cooled sufficiently, the moulds were lifted off and prepared for re-use. This operation does not need to be adjacent to the melting shop. It frequently was, as I have modelled it, but it was not always the case.

Several rail lines run into the ends of these buildings. Lines carry steel scrap into the stockyard bay, possibly on a raised gantry, others, which serve the casting bay, deliver liquid iron from the blast furnaces and carry slag traffic and ingot casting cars.

Some melting shops are equipped with tilting open-hearth furnaces. Without labouring the detail, they impact on the rail service provided as they require slag ladles to be delivered from the side, under the mezzanine floor. I have adopted this feature to add even more railway interest.

The No.1 melting shop at Lancashire Steel looking at the then recently extended scrap bay. The row of chimneys, brick here, is a signal feature of an open-hearth melting shop.
TATA STEEL EUROPE

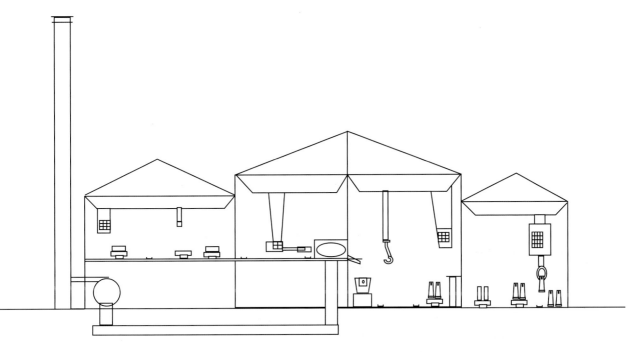

A cross-section of a typical open-hearth melting shop. The furnaces are end on, aligned along the edge of the charging floor. The underground flue links them to the waste heat boilers and chimneys. Overhead type furnace chargers are shown.

THE PROJECT BUILD

The project build is intended to represent a typical melting shop, of the type built in the 1950s at a number of the UKs steelworks and, as with other project builds, it will eventually form a key component of a large model steelworks. To facilitate this, and because of its size, a strong sub-baseboard was constructed. Framed and supported by thin, plywood strips, three panels of 5mm foamboard were laminated together to provide a strong and level base. This module will jigsaw fit with similar surrounding modules to build up the complete works.

Though melting shops have some unique features, the modelling techniques used in the build translate readily to any large, panel-clad, industrial building. The basic structure is constructed from foamboard, in 5 and 10mm thicknesses, which is then clad in textured plastic sheet. For this build, the sheet used represents corrugated iron though, if appropriate, sheet repre-

senting either corrugated asbestos or more modern box-section cladding could be used.

Whatever the nature of the prototype chosen, these buildings are large and few modellers will have the space available to model one to scale. For the project, a space was allocated for the footprint of the building and the height developed to give both the right sense of proportion and to allow the required rail access at the gable end. To save space, and to allow an easier approach for the railway lines, the building is built at an angle to, and into, the back-scene. The building is modelled in partial relief and the model represents roughly half of its notional length. As it stands, the building is 1.5m (5ft) long and 0.7m (2.5ft) wide.

Having decided on a footprint and the ridge heights for the building, a start was made in cutting out the profile formers in 10mm foamboard. These were cut to span the full width of the building and to include the three distinct roof ridgelines. When marking these out it is important to take account

of the thickness of the sidewalls so that the overall building finishes at the designed size.

Apertures were also cut for the rail access points and to allow the lines to run, at least partway, into the building. At the ridges a 10mm-wide slot, 50mm deep, was also cut.

These formers were then accurately aligned on the baseboard, glued down with PVA and supported with foamboard brackets. Lengths of 10mm foamboard were fitted into the pre-cut ridge slots. These were fitted to help with alignment, to support the profiles and also to later support the roof itself. The profile formers and the ridge supports were left overnight for the PVA to fully harden. Strips of foamboard, 50mm wide, were then cut to fit between the profile formers to provide support for the side-walls. Without this bracing there is the possibility that the side-walls might bow in or out between the formers. Similar bracing was fixed anywhere a long span of side-wall or roofing might need support.

The position of the formers had not been pre-determined with reference to the slag rail lines coming in from the side. These lines were now fitted and the foamboard cut away as required. They are just short, curved lines and will later be extended

to join a slag road running parallel with the melting shop. The whole interior was sprayed with matt black automotive paint so that all of that white foamboard will be lost in the internal gloom.

Attention was next turned to the side-walls and roof panels, which were all cut from 5mm foamboard. The main side-wall required a number of apertures cutting into it. These included open doorways for the railway lines, smaller personnel doorways at different levels and a space at the lower right where a brick office block was to be partially built into the melting shop. Melting shop sides often featured large, open ventilation gaps and these, five groups of six, were also cut out.

The side and roof panels were dry-assembled using masking tape just to check for size and fit. Before cladding was applied to the roof panels, 20mm-wide strips of 10mm foamboard were stuck using UHU along the ridge lines; these will form the clerestory vents, a feature commonly seen on industrial buildings. The cladding itself is Slater's corrugated styrene applied in overlapping strips, as outlined in Chapter 5. On the roof panels, the cladding overlapped the lower edge and the ends by 5mm, and was fitted up to the clerestory strip. The narrow, upper side-

Preparing the profile formers with the rail access points marked out.

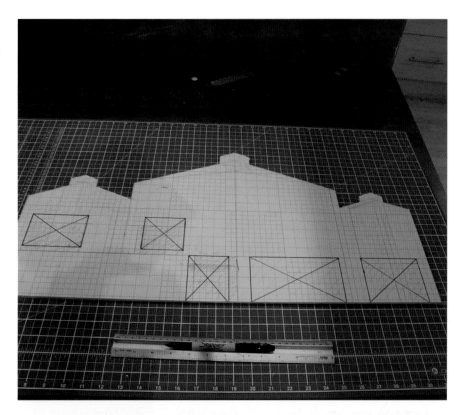

The formers fitted, the spine running along the nearside ridge is visible and railway lines are trial fitted.

walls of the melting shop were clad next. They too were allowed a 5mm overlap, this time along the top edge. When the walls and roof panels are fitted together, the edge of the roof sits on the side-walls. The extended cladding at the top of the walls covers the exposed edge of the roof foamboard, while the extended cladding on the roof forms the eaves overhang. Once clad, the roof panels and side-walls were attached to the main building carcass using PVA. The gable end-walls, formed by the end profile formers, were clad in place, with care being taken to ensure that the horizontal lines of the cladding were level either side of the open doorways. Some excess cladding is allowed at each doorway or opening and is cut back to form a neat opening later.

Guttering and downpipes will be added later from 'c' channel and styrene rod.

As there was a reasonable amount of detail to be added on the main side-wall, this was fixed while the wall was still flat. Access openings for the slag roads were tidied up and supporting steelwork, made up from paired Evergreen truss girders, positioned just inside, either side of the doorway. Holes were drilled in the side-wall for the chimney flues using a 20mm spade bit in a drill. The bit needs to be rotating at a high speed and introduced to the wall very slowly and very carefully. Each of the wall-mounted pipe racks was a simple construction from lengths of Evergreen section, with the pipe-supporting saddles made as outlined in the pipework section in Chapter 5.

The larger diameter pipe was made up from Plastruct 12mm tubing, scribed into sections using a pipe cutter, with the bends, flanges and T-fittings made up from Plastruct fittings. The large valve fitted on the scrap bay end-wall is made up from a Plastruct T and flanges, and detailed with styrene discs and sections. Non-branded styrene tube bought from China via eBay formed the smaller lower pipe. A Knightwing piping kit supplied bends and valves that drop down from the main pipe and feed into the melting shop wall. All of this pipework is 'imagineered' using photographs for guidance and inspiration.

The construction of the chimneys was covered and illustrated in Chapter 5. They will remain a tem-

With the formers and base painted matt black, some of the extra longitudinal support ribs stand out in white.

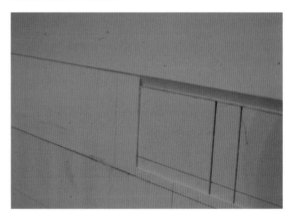

Cladding at the top of the walls extends upwards so that it covers the exposed foam edge of the roof panels.

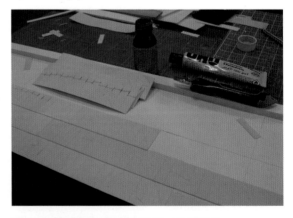

The roof being clad. A strip of 10mm foamboard was glued along the upper edge of each roof panel to form a base for the clerestory vent.

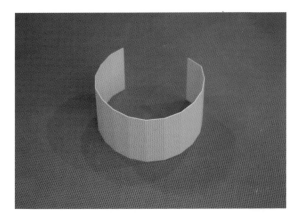

A prepared cladding strip. By carefully bending it around, the vertical joints open up a little.

The rear wall of the melting shop showing the dwarf wall and the cladding primed ready for painting.

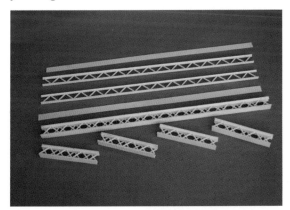

Plastruct truss girders glued back to back make useful structural members. These were positioned vertically just inside each doorway.

porary fit until the whole building is installed on the main layout.

The sides of the clerestory vents were made up with styrene strips to look something like the vents seen on the Mitchell & Shackleton building illustrated in Chapter 2. These took a while to make up and each vent side was completed in a single piece. They consist of four lengths of 40 thou strip, 10mm wide, spaced apart by narrow strips of 80 thou strip. Once fitted, the clerestory tops were clad in corrugated styrene with a strip of masking tape used to form a ridge cover.

Sometimes brick buildings are constructed within the footprint of these large, metal-clad structures. These buildings will generally house offices or small workshops, they will have external windows and, if more than one storey, may feature external stairways. I wanted to incorporate such a feature in the melting shop model and planned for a workshop for the melting shop maintenance fitters to sit in one corner. I built a simple, single-story industrial building using embossed styrene over a foamboard shell. It is fitted with Scalelink etched windows, a large sliding door and a small personnel door.

Half of it stands outside the main structure, which has a flat, concrete roof. The other half is modelled within one corner of the main structure; however, this is an illusion. The outer front wall of the workshop just extends into a space left behind the main

A sample of the roof vents, fabricated in white styrene, sits on top of the clerestory. Beneath it a length of painted vent can be seen in place.

The fitter's workshop showing how it slides into the main structure. The brickwork sheet extends to include part of the dwarf wall so that there is no visible join.

The completed open-hearth melting shop.

A Yorkshire Engine Company DE2 shunter removes empty scrap pans from the stockyard.

building's cladding and matches up with the dwarf wall brickwork. The photographs will make this arrangement much clearer.

The final fitting was the gantries bringing the rail line up to the scrap and charging bay floor levels; the ones shown in the photographs may be temporary. On the final installation the rail lines will initially rise up on a single earthwork embankment, they will then part and pass along two lengths of structural steel bridgework and into the melting shop. It may well prove simpler to re-build them all at the same time. In the meantime the temporary, short gantries give an idea of the final arrangement. They have 10mm foamboard cores with structural 'steel' outers made up from styrene sheet and Plastruct sections. The deck is covered in a chequerplate pattern embossed styrene sheet with the rail lines on top.

The metal water-tower described in Chapter 12 stands at the side of the melting shop and will be linked to it with a stairway.

Groundcover is dry pointing mortar mix held down with PVA; weathering powders add a little extra texture. A concrete roadway runs into the side of the melting shop to give access to, amongst other things, the refractory brick store within: in turn, the furnaces were being rebuilt and relined continually.

Some of the more delicate details, e.g. handrails and walkways, have been omitted or minimized for the present. They would be a little vulnerable whilst such a large structure is in storage. The railway lines serving the end of the building and the ground cover is temporary. Both will be fixed and blended in when the adjacent boards are fitted.

The access roadway leading under the charging floor.

Some walkways, stairways and a large valve with access platform.

The fitter's office and workshop with the water tower support structure to the left.

A corner of industry, the open doorway of the workshop with the rail gantry above.

CONCLUSION

That completes the largest single project in the book. A small, shunting layout could be housed within. Despite referring to them as large, black sheds, I actually chose to paint this in a washed-out green. Buildings in this colour stood at the steelworks at Ebbw Vale and at Dorman Longs' works on Teesside.

The paint used was from the Tamiya acrylic range and is called 'Sky'. I have to say, if I saw the sky that colour I'd be running for the hills. Nonetheless, it worked well. I purposely applied it in a thin coat to give it a slightly faded look from a distance. Some minimal weathering was applied but I need to take the building outdoors to do it properly. That will be done in the spring.

CHAPTER FIFTEEN

LOCOMOTIVES, ROLLING STOCK AND VEHICLES

INTRODUCTION

I don't intend to include blow-by-blow accounts of the building or modifying of rail and road vehicles in this volume. There are plenty of other books, including several from The Crowood Press, covering locomotive and rolling-stock kit construction and the modification of 'ready-to-run' models. What I do want to do is discuss the provision of industrial locomotives, and rolling stock in particular, and the assembly of a road fleet appropriate to a model industry.

THE PROTOTYPE

LOCOMOTIVES

The very earliest steam locomotives were built to serve the needs of industrial concerns and over the following years, thousands of locomotives have been built for, and seen service at, countless indus-

trial sites. The UK was unusual in that almost all of the mainline railway companies employed their own locomotive designers and built locomotives in their own workshops. In many other countries, locomotives were bought from private builders, sometimes to railway company designs, sometimes as standard off-the-shelf designs. As a consequence, the UK's private locomotive builders concentrated on building locomotives for export and supplying the needs of the countless domestic industrial customers. To protect their interests, the mainline companies were prohibited from building and selling locomotives into this market, though some second-hand mainline locomotives were sold on for service in industry.

ROLLING STOCK

Within the confines of an industrial site on the internal railway system, there will be examples of mainline rolling-stock. The type of stock, and the amount of it, will naturally reflect the needs of the industry in

One of Hornby's Peckett W4 saddle tanks repainted to suit the steelworks fleet.

A pair of large Yorkshire Engine Company 0-6-0 saddle tanks built from etched kits.

A work-begrimed Sentinel built from an RT Models' kit.

Typical steel works' shunting power: Yorkshire Engine Company DE2 shunters built from Judith Edge kits. The different pattern of wasp striping reflects the company's developing livery.

terms of its raw material usage and product output. Most of these wagons will be the common, run of the mill, mineral wagons, opens, flats and box vans. However, the industry might also see more specialized vehicles, such as hoppers, steel-carrying bolsters and plate wagons, tank wagons, grain hoppers; in fact any wagon you wish to run, just choose the right industry. One of the benefits of including heavy industry on a layout is the excuse to run some of these unusual and specialized vehicles. One of the prototype photographs in Chapter 9, overhead cranes, illustrates a large Flatrol EAA wagon; they don't come much more specialized than that.

There is also the possibility of featuring specialized rolling-stock found in industry and not seen on the main lines. The iron and steel industry, in particular, employed some highly specialized types of rolling stock. Many industries also operated railway-mounted cranes, of which there was a bewildering variety. Some were combined 'locomotive cranes', which could be hand-, steam- or diesel-powered and ranged in lifting capacity from a ton to in excess of one hundred tons. Ransomes and Rapier of Ipswich supplied a heavy breakdown crane to the Steel Company of Wales at Port Talbot in the 1950s, which was, at the time, the largest railway crane in the UK.

ROAD VEHICLES AND PLANT

Road vehicles have become universally present at industrial sites. Before World War II they were not too common but all that was to change with the huge growth in road transport from the 1950s onwards. Lorries started to be used for both internal and external transport needs, with companies building up their own fleets or employing outside contractors, usually both. Some internal departments might be allocated their own road vehicles. Engineering and maintenance teams might have the use of their own lorries, vans or cars for use on site.

Though car ownership expanded considerably, private cars driving around large industrial sites were, and remain, uncommon. Central car-parking facilities are usually provided rather than allowing cars free access over the internal roadways. This is partly from safety concerns and partly from a desire to minimize congestion. This should be borne in mind when positioning private cars on a model of an industrial site – keep them to a minimum. Very large sites might provide their own internal bus service. As an example, the steelworks at Shotton had a large fleet of buses that ferried workers from a bus station by the main gate to various parts of the plant at shift changeover times. During the shifts, one or

A Ruston 165DE, modified from a Judith Edge kit. It will eventually serve the by-product plant.

A pair of Janus shunters, these from Judith Edge kits, but soon to be available ready to run from Golden Valley Models.

two buses circled the works, providing transport for those needing it.

Various examples of specialized plant might also be present, e.g. cranes, bulldozers, loaders and excavators; just whatever would be dictated by the needs of the industry. Consider also emergency vehicles, such as works' police vehicles, fire engines and ambulances. In the 1930s, the managing director of Lancashire Steel passed on his old Rolls-Royce to the company and it was converted into a works' ambulance.

MODELS

LOCOMOTIVES

The modeller relying on 'ready-to-run' models has, until recently, had a limited choice in terms of suitable locomotives for use on an industrial layout. Some mainline prototypes could be pressed into service, just as they had been in real life. The Stroudley Terrier, the L&Y Pug, the LMS 'Jinty' 0-6-0T and the BR 03 and 08 diesel shunters are all prototypes that have been available RTR and which saw some industrial use, but they were hardly typical.

Several years ago Dapol introduced their model of an Austerity tank locomotive, the 0-6-0ST used by the LNER, and later BR, known as the J94. Introduced as a

standard wartime design, many hundreds were used by industry in the post-war years, by the National Coal Board in particular. As an industrial locomotive it was fine as far as it went but it was a big locomotive suited only to the largest industrial sites.

Things have much improved. In 2013, Hornby released a model of the chain-drive Sentinel 0-4-0DH, a locomotive that only ever saw industrial service. It was followed by a model of the similar coupling-rod driven Sentinel. Just being delivered at the end of 2016 is the first purely industrial steam outline locomotive, Hornby's W4 Peckett 0-4-0ST; and a lovely little model it is too. Judging by many favourable comments it has been very well-received and may well spur some into a first foray into industrial modelling. Its success may also see further industrials from the major manufacturers. Golden Valley Models have commissioned Oxford Models to produce a Yorkshire Engine Company 'Janus' 0-6-0DE, a long-lived prototype widely used in the steel industry and elsewhere. Like the Austerity saddle tank, these are large locomotives by industrial standards but very well-suited to heavy industry. The Golden Valley model should be available about the same time that this book hits the shelves. DJM have announced that they will produce a model of a Hudswell Clarke 0-6-0ST. For the first time, modelling a convincing

Specialized rolling-stock. Ingot buggies with large ingot moulds being propelled out of the melting shop.

It doesn't get more specialized than this – a torpedo ladle for moving liquid iron heavily rebuilt from Walters' kits to represent a UK design.

industrial locomotive fleet purely from RTR sources is becoming possible.

For the modeller prepared to venture into kit-building there is a very wide range of prototypes available in model form. Some of the finest etched kits available are those of industrial prototypes in the large Judith Edge Range, mainly of diesel prototypes, from High Level Kits, largely of steam prototypes, and RT Models with their Sentinels and others. Other manufacturers over the years have included Impetus, sadly long gone, Agenoria, Wychbury and CPS. These ranges have changed hands over the years but can usually be found with a little searching. Not surprisingly, the largest range is in 4mm scale, though there are also many in 7mm scale.

ROLLING STOCK

Some industries used second-hand mainline rolling-stock for their needs, while others bought mainline designs from new. The colliery companies had large fleets of wooden bodied coal wagons and the National Coal Board had large fleets of steel mineral wagons in their internal fleets. The Manchester Ship Canal Company also had a large fleet of wooden open wagons. For specialized rolling-stock the modeller has to turn to kits or scratchbuilding. For the steel industry modeller, US companies like Walthers

Part of the steelworks' road fleet parked up handily for the canteen.

Some of the full fleet, some modified Basetoys, some modified Oxford Diecast with much scratchbuilding.

and STD have offered specialized vehicles in their ranges and these, with a little modification, are suitable for UK locations. RT Models in the UK also have a number of useful industrial wagons in their range, including a typically British slag ladle and the Hudson 'V' side-tipping wagon, as used in several industries.

ROAD VEHICLES

A number of model suppliers have offered road vehicle kits in their ranges over the years and one of the largest, mainly of lorries, was available from Langley Models. These are cast white-metal kits, which made up very well and offered many useful models for the 1950s and 1960s, in particular. They were joined by Road Transport Images who offer a very large range of lorries with models suitable for the 1930s through to the present day. RTI kits are cast resin and follow a modular concept in that the cabs, wheels, chassis and bodies are sold separately and then combined to produce whatever vehicle is required. The cabs, in particular, are useful in modifying the enormous range of commercial vehicles that

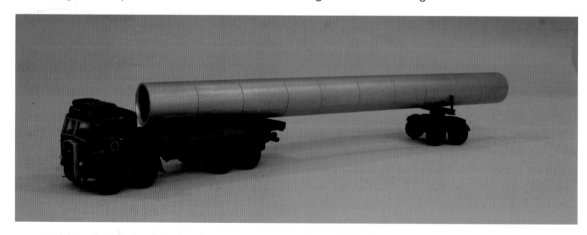

A combination you would not see on today's roads: a venerable Atkinson eight-wheeler, with a dolly trailer, carrying a long load. Securing chains will be fitted at some stage.

A contractor's short wheelbase Foden tipper is spotted parked up behind the laboratory.

have poured out from suppliers like EFE, Pocketbond, Basetoys and Oxford in recent years. Most of them capture the look of their prototypes very well, a few less so, and some are a little under scale. They provide a quick and inexpensive way to acquire a fleet of commercial vehicles and plant with which to populate any industry. With the will to set about modifying them, an interesting and unique collection is eminently possible.

CONCLUSION

I've illustrated some of my own railway and road fleets. The locomotive fleet was built up on the availability of models from kits, and more recently from the likes of Hornby, and which matched the types of locomotives that saw service in the steel industry. For example, the Yorkshire Engine Company, which was owned by the United Steel Company, supplied large numbers to the steel industry. As a consequence, I have six in my steelworks' fleet. Rolling stock represents the typical

collection of ladle- and ingot-carrying vehicles, along with some less specialized vehicles. The road fleet has largely maintained an allegiance to one builder: Leyland. Leyland was considered a maker of premium commercial vehicles back in 1960 and many industrial concerns would have been loyal to one supplier. The steelworks' fleet consists of four-, six- and eight-wheel Leyland rigid lorries and two Scammell tractor units with articulated trailers. The works' internal road fleet is made up from Fordson and Ford lorries. All the fleets are tied together with a common livery and are lettered with some custom decals. I have tried to represent changing times. The diesel fleet livery has no lining and uses a simplified lettering. Both steam and diesel locomotives show variation in the amount of wasp striping on their ends. This reflects a trend within the industry to make the locomotives ever more visible, yet all locomotives would not be repainted at the same time.

It's your fleet, you are in charge, develop it to reflect your own interests.

CHAPTER SIXTEEN

HEAVY INDUSTRY IN SMALL SPACES

INTRODUCTION

Heavy industry and small spaces are unusual bed-fellows. The very definition of heavy industry, one of high investment, suggests a large site likely to be covering several acres. An acre, if square, would be a little over 200 x 200ft or 800 x 800mm in 4mm scale. An industry covering just 20 acres, and that is small in heavy industry terms, would need an area, say, 8 x 1.6m in 4mm scale. Many of the models described in this book are large, with the melting shop alone covering an area on which a small layout could be built.

POMONA WORKS

However, railway modellers are a creative bunch and attempting to squeeze a quart into a pint pot is a familiar challenge. The essence of heavy industry can be suggested in a surprisingly small space.

The model featured in the first two photographs occupies an area of less than 6 square feet. It was built to try out some constructional techniques and has since functioned as a module on which items of rolling stock can be posed and photographed. Though one end was never fully completed, it demonstrates that a model just a few inches deep, 10in (25cm) in this case, can suggest the presence of heavy industry and provide some industrial railway operating opportunities. The building shown differs from the melting shop built in Chapter 15 in that instead of using scribed strips of corrugated styrene, it was clad using Wills corrugated iron sheets.

These sheets can work well enough but they do take a bit of extra work. The horizontal jointing issue was overcome on this model by running pipework along the joints and by breaking up the vertical space with a row of windows. These strategies work but they also introduce some limitations for how a building can be developed.

The Pomona module. A Yorkshire Engine Company 'Janus' shunter moves ingots from the stripping bay.

Wills corrugated iron sheeting was used on the Pomona buildings. The pipework and row of windows helps disguise the horizontal joints.

The entire Staplegrove module, 3ft wide by 2ft deep.

STAPLEGROVE MODULE

This module was built for the RMWeb South Western Area Group's annual exhibition and meeting, which has been held in Staplegrove, Taunton, for the past few years. The module measures 3 x 2ft and is 1ft tall. It is built on a foamboard baseboard, supported on ply strip and housed in an open-fronted box. The box protects the module during transportation and storage, and was made from some melamine-faced chipboard that I had lying around. As the module was built to be portable it was finished off with a lid and fitted with carrying handles. Again, this was built to test out some more building techniques and to provide a more modern backdrop on which to photograph some of my 1970s' industrial vehicles. The two main lines along the front can be linked to modules brought along by other modeller's to provide a long run. The industrial lines, those behind the fencing, are not wired up. It was never intended to be a working module, though by providing short fiddle yards or sidings for the lines to run on to as they exit the module, it could provide some interesting shunting operations.

The main buildings are all built on foamboard shells using Slater's corrugated styrene sheeting prepared in exactly the same way as those used in the melting shop project in Chapter 15.

An Atkinson 'Leader' drives out of the 18in mill laden with steel billets. The model is a conversion from an Oxford Diecast tractor unit with a scratchbuilt trailer.

In fact, many of the constructional techniques described in this book were pioneered and developed on this project. The lessons learned in modelling the pipework, roadways, walkways and stairways, amongst others, were applied to the projects already described. Montana matt paints were used to paint the large buildings and the 'BSC STAPLEGROVE WORKS' lettering and logo were created with desktop publishing and printed as decals by Precision Decals.

The module demonstrates that by modelling buildings in partial relief, an impressive industrial complex can be suggested in a small space. The large building across the back is only 2in (5cm) deep and, with the railway line directly in front, both are just 4in (10cm) deep. Including a boundary fence, a large building and a functional industrial line could be featured and take up no more than 3 or 4in at the rear of a layout. The rear building also demonstrates its potential as a rear backdrop, there being no need for a painted one. The buildings on either side illustrate the possibilities for corner filling with industrial buildings, again with railway access and the associated operating potential.

The large building includes a feature seen in the photograph of the Landore Foundry in Chapter 2: a lower corner has been cut back to clear a railway

The cutaway corner of the rear building allows a rail line to curve out towards the rear of the module. A repainted Hornby Sentinel shunts a train of bogie bolster wagons.

A quiet moment at Staplegrove. Caught over the fence, Sentinel DH3 idles away outside the soaking pits building.

line as it curves around. It is little details like this that add interest and, just like the prototype, allow more to be squeezed in.

CONCLUSION

Staplegrove combines modified readymade resin buildings with some completely scratchbuilt structures and demonstrates how they can be brought together in a cohesive manner. As the testbed for a future, much larger, project, it proved invaluable in developing techniques for working with a range of materials and constructing large industrial structures. Many of the methods employed in the building of both Pomona Works and Staplegrove Works led directly to the building of the projects in this book. Both of them demonstrate the possibilities for heavy industry in small spaces.

CHAPTER SEVENTEEN

CONCLUSION

I hope the preceding chapters have provided both interest and inspiration for the modelling of heavy industry. Either as a simple backdrop or as a barn-filling recreation of a major industry, the techniques covered should help in the planning and construction. My own model captures a slice of history — many of the structures modelled no longer exist in this country, either because technology has moved on or moved elsewhere. The writing of this book, with deadlines to meet, certainly spurred me on and also encouraged me to look for ways to speed up jobs.

And finally, cats — did you spot them? There are cats featured in three of the completed model project photographs. Feral and semi-feral cats found many sites of heavy industry an ideal home. There were tens of them roaming around Irlam Steelworks, each usually having its own little territory and, as they kept vermin under control, no attempt was made to round them up and remove them. Along with any vermin they caught, there was other wildlife on site, scraps from the canteen and many of the men fed them. They were welcomed into some of the mess rooms scattered about the plant and there was always some warm cranny to sleep in. It wasn't always a safe environment, being filled with obvious, and some not so obvious, hazards, but the population seemed to thrive. I know from talking to others who worked in large industrial environments that they too had their own cat populations.

So where are they?

There's one snoozing on the roof of the melting shop fitters' building, the rumble of passing trains seems to be of little concern.

Another waits hopefully by the rear doors of the canteen.

The third sits watching the activity in the roll shop front yard.

They're made from Milliput and wire.

RESOURCES FOR MODELLERS

FURTHER READING

Little is readily available new in book format and I can only recommend scouring second-hand sources for literature covering your favoured industry. The Industrial Railway Society (see below), have a number of books available that cover industrial railways and that contain information about the relevant industries. There are some magazines that can provide information and inspiration.

Archive magazine
Black Dwarf Lightmoor
120 Farmers Close
Witney
Oxfordshire OX28 1NR
http://www.lightmoor.co.uk
A quarterly magazine devoted to industrial and transport history.

Railway Bylines magazine
Irwell Press Ltd
59A High Street
Clophill
Bedfordshire MK45 4BE
http://www.irwellpress.co.uk
This is published monthly, and routinely has articles on industrial railways and the industries they served.

Kelsey Media
Kelsey Publishing Ltd
Cudham Tithe Barn
Berry's Hill
Cudham
Kent TN16 3AG
http://kelsey.co.uk

Publishers of a series of 'bookazines', *Moving the Goods*, which have looked at the railways and a number of specific industries, coal, car-making, steel, etc. and which are still available at the time of writing.

Industrial Railway Society
S. C. Robinson (Membership Secretary)
47 Waverley Gardens
London NW10 7EE
http://www.irsociety.co.uk
Membership brings a regular copy of the IRS publication, the Industrial Railway Record, which covers industrial railways, their locomotives and the industries they served. The society also publishes a wide range of books on the same topics.

LIST OF SUPPLIERS

It is always good to support your local model shop whenever possible and it is worth mentioning that model shops specializing in aeronautical and maritime modelling often have good stocks of useful and interesting model-making materials.

Here is a list of some suppliers which the modeller of heavy industry might find useful.

The Airbrush Company
79 Marlborough Road
Lancing Business Park
Lancing
West Sussex BN15 8UF
http://www.airbrushes.com
Airbrushes, compressors paint and other airbrushing supplies.

Alan Gibson
PO Box 597,

Oldham OL1 9FQ
http://www.alangibsonworkshop.com
Etched brass water-tank panels, metal wires and a huge range of locomotive and rolling stock parts.

Cad4trading
La Ronde Complet
Market Road
Bradwell
Norfolk NR31 9EB
www.cad4trading.com
Suppliers of larger sheets of styrene and other modelling plastics.

Crafty Computer Paper
Woodhall
Barrasford
Hexham
Northumberland NE48 4DB
http://www.craftycomputerpaper.co.uk
Waterslide decal paper for the home printing of decals.

Eileen's Emporium
Unit 19, 1 Highnam Business Centre
Newent Road
Gloucester GL2 8DN
http://www.eileensemporium.com
Tools and modelling materials, including Evergreen and Plastruct.

EMA Model Supplies Ltd
14 Beadman Street
London SE27 0DN
http://www.ema-models.co.uk
Suppliers of a wide range of architectural modelling supplies, including the complete Plastruct range.

Evergreen Scale Models
http://www.evergreenscalemodels.com
Suppliers of styrene strip, sheet and section. Evergreen is stocked at many UK model shops and suppliers but this link will enable modeller's to see what is available.

Freestone Model Accessories
Newland Mill,
Witney
Oxfordshire
http://freestonemodel.co.uk
Suppliers of a large range of architectural modelling supplies largely, though not exclusively, for building in card.

High Level Models
High Level Kits
14 Tudor Road
Chester-le-Street
County Durham DH3 3RY
http://www.highlevelkits.co.uk
Manufacturers of etched brass industrial locomotive kits and suppliers of motors and gearboxes.

Judith Edge Kits
5 Chapel Lane
Carlton
Barnsley
South Yorkshire S71 3LE
http://www.ukmodelshops.co.uk
Manufacturers of etched brass industrial locomotive kits and parts.

Langley Models
166 Three Bridges Road,
Three Bridges
Crawley
West Sussex RH10 1LE
http://www.langleymodels.com
Manufacturers of a range of cast white-metal road vehicles, and cast and etched buildings and details.

Metcalfe Models & Toys Ltd
Bell Busk
Skipton
North Yorkshire BD23 4DU
http://metcalfemodels.com
Manufacturers of printed card building kits and brick and other textured printed papers.

Peach Creek Shops
2405 Blue Valley Drive
Silver Spring
Maryland 20904
USA
http://www.peachcreekshops.com
US-based supplier of steel mill related kits, parts and
information.

PPD Ltd
Unit 3, Highbank Park
Lochgilphead
Argyll PA31 8NN
http://www.ppdltd.com
Custom brass etching service.

Precision Labels/PrecisionDecals
07800 744170
http://www.precisionlabels.com
Suppliers of decals and a custom decal printing
service.

Road Transport Images
17 Foxdene Road
Seasalter
Whitstable
Kent CT5 4QY
http://www.roadtransportimages.com
Suppliers of resin kits for complete lorries along with
a range of related components.

RT Models
75 Yew Tree Close
Spring Gardens
Shrewsbury
Shropshire SY1 2UR
http://www.rtmodels.co.uk
A source of industrial locomotives, wagons and
industrial detailing parts.

Scalescenes
http://www.scalescenes.com
A range of building kits and brick papers, which are
purchased online and then printed off, at home, as
many times as the modeller requires.

Sign Materials Direct
97 Kingsley Road
Hounslow
Middlesex TW3 4AH
http://www.signmaterialsdirect.com
Wholesalers and internet suppliers of a range of
foamboards in different colours and sizes.

Skytex Ltd
Unit 1 Charnwood Business Park
North Road
Loughborough
Leicestershire LE11 1LE
http://www.skytrexmodelrailways.com
Manufacturers of cast resin buildings including chim-
neys and warehouse walls.

Slater's Plasticard
Old Road
Darley Dale
Matlock
Derbyshire DE4 2ER
http://www.slatersplasticard.com
Plasticard brand styrene sheet and section amongst
other modelling supplies.

Squires Model & Craft Tools
100 London Road
Bognor Regis
West Sussex PO21 1DD
http://www.squirestools.com
Tools and modelling materials including Evergreen
and Plastruct.

INDEX